New Dimensions of Project Management

Arthur D. Little Books

A series of books on management and other scientific and technical subjects by senior professional staff members of Arthur D. Little, Inc., the international consulting and research organization. The series also includes selected nonproprietary case studies.

Acquisition and Corporate Development   James W. Bradley and Donald H. Korn

Bankruptcy Risk in Financial Depository Intermediaries: Assessing Regulatory Effects   Michael F. Koehn

Board Compass: What It Means to Be a Director in a Changing World   Robert Kirk Mueller

Career Conflict: Management's Inelegant Dysfunction   Robert Kirk Mueller

The Corporate Development Process   Anthony J. Marolda

Corporate Responsibilities and Opportunities to 1990   Ellen T. Curtiss and Philip A. Untersee

The Dynamics of Industrial Location: Microeconometric Modeling for Policy Analysis   Kirkor Bozdogan and David Wheeler

Systems Methods for Socioeconomic and Environmental Impact Analysis   Glenn R. De Souza

The Incompleat Board: The Unfolding of Corporate Governance   Robert Kirk Mueller

Energy Policy and Forecasting   Glenn R. De Souza

Communications Network Analysis   Howard Cravis

Board Score: How to Judge Boardworthiness   Robert Kirk Mueller

International Telecommunications: User Requirements and Supplier Strategies   Edited by Kathleen Landis Lancaster

New Dimensions of Project Management   Edited by Albert J. Kelley

Wind Power for the Electric-Utility Industry: Policy Incentives for Fuel Conservation   Frederic March, Edward H. Dlott, Donald H. Korn, Frederick R. Madio, Robert C. McArthur, and William A. Vachon

New Dimensions of Project Management

Edited by
Albert J. Kelley
Arthur D. Little Program
Systems Management Company

An Arthur D. Little Book

LexingtonBooks
D.C. Heath and Company
Lexington, Massachusetts
Toronto

Library of Congress Cataloging in Publication Data

Main entry under title:

New dimensions of project management.

    Papers derived from the seminar in Boston, Apr. 6–7, 1981, organized by
the Arthur D. Little Program Systems Management Company.
    Includes index.
    1. Industrial project management—Congresses. I. Kelley, Albert J.
II. Arthur D. Little Program Systems Management Company.

HD69.P75N48	658.4'04	81–47969
ISBN 0–669–05190–x		AACR2

Second printing, September 1983

Published simultaneously in Canada

Printed in the United States of America

International Standard Book Number: 0–669–05190–x

Library of Congress Catalog Card Number: 81–47969

Contents

Preface and Acknowledgments

In the 1980s we face tough and increasingly complex challenges in managing major capital-investment projects. Significant changes in the nature of projects and the environment in which they are managed are occurring every day, and there are more and larger projects than ever before. Industry and government are turning to uniquely identifiable projects or programs rather than treating the management of such efforts as permanent administrative undertakings. Many of these projects are assuming a size and technical complexity unparalleled in the history of project management. The special category of large international projects involving sophisticated concepts and highly competitive conditions also continues to grow at a fast rate. The multinational and sometimes remote character of such projects compounds the project-management task even further. Several other factors have had a pronounced impact on project management in recent years, and major complications can be expected to continue in the next decade:

1. Projects are more constrained by such external factors as the ecological-societal environment; state, local, and federal regulatory considerations; and the multiple management interests of owners, financiers, and project executors.
2. Cost overruns are forcing greater assurance that projects will be completed on schedule.
3. Advanced technology and unproved methods are introducing significant new unknowns and risks in many projects.
4. Economic volatility and increasing inflationary pressures are producing special problems in financing projects and in coping with the dynamics of the financial environment.

This overview of the trends in project management makes it clear to see that managing projects in the 1980s already is extremely difficult, and it is expected to become even more demanding. Planning and executing a capital-intensive project within scope, schedule, and cost objectives will require broader, more advanced management skills than ever before and more attention to strategic and external factors over the life of the project.

The impetus for this book was an awareness that corporate, project, and investment managers need to understand and cope better with the project-management environment of the 1980s. In late 1980, Arthur D. Little

Program Systems Management Company, an operating unit of Arthur D. Little, Inc., Cambridge, Massachusetts, organized a seminar entitled "New Dimensions of Project Management—Challenge for the 1980s." Contributors were drawn from a cross section of international project-management experts, representing experience in industry, government, and academia. Their individual topics were chosen to provide intensive, forward-looking examinations of the key problem areas and the issues discussed earlier. The seminar was held in Boston on 6–7 April 1981, and the chapters in this book were derived from the contents of that seminar.

In part I, "Introduction and Overview," chapter 1 sets the stage by providing a broad look at the history of project management and where it appears to be headed. John F. Magee, president and chief executive officer of Arthur D. Little, Inc., shares some of his perceptions on the relevance of project management in the coming decade, and outlines the purpose and theme of the book. In chapter 2, I outline the elements that characterize the new project environment of the 1980s. This overview, which points out the complexity and dynamic nature of the new project environment, establishes the basic premise for chapters to follow.

Part II, "Policy and Environment," provides detailed discussions of four topics bearing on the issues associated with policy, environment, and external factors. In chapter 3, Mel Horwitch, of Sloan School of Management, Massachusetts Institute of Technology, and C.K. Prahalad, of the Graduate School of Business Administration, University of Michigan, examine the unique problems in managing large-scale public or private enterprises. Chapter 4 covers the regulatory and socioeconomic issues in major projects. James S. Hoyte, vice-president of Arthur D. Little Program Systems Management Company, focuses his discussion on the impact of local, state, and federal regulations and legal requirements; the socioeconomic setting of the project; and citizen participation. Chapter 5 deals with what James Costantino, director of the Transportation Systems Center, U.S. Department of Transportation, calls the "changing federal perspective" with respect to research and development projects. Chapter 6 closes part II with an examination of the impacts of innovation and technology on managing projects. Robert C. Seamans, Jr., dean of engineering at the Massachusetts Institute of Technology, looks at some project examples and the roles of industry and government in developing his outlook for the 1980s.

Part III, "Strategy and Planning," consists of three chapters that deal with factors affecting the formulation of large projects under the conditions of uncertainty found in the environment of the 1980s. Chapter 7 is devoted to development of strategy considerations regarding the project and its relation to the corporation. John R. White, senior vice-president of Arthur D.

Little, Inc., explains how the key characteristics of various categories of projects influence the strategies of competitors in the field. In chapter 8, Karl M. Wiig, of the Operations Research Section, Arthur D. Little, Inc., treats in considerable detail the subject of planning for uncertainty in large projects. He offers and describes three representative tools for this purpose. Finally, project financing is covered in chapter 9 by Theodore V. Fowler, director of the Project Finance Group, The First Boston Corporation. He traces the delicate process of project financing, pointing out that, in the economic climate of the 1980s, more attention must be given to project financing at an earlier stage in the planning of projects.

Part IV, "Project Control and Risk Management," is a four-chapter section that examines the issues of risk with respect to large projects and examines the emerging new needs for management control. In chapter 10, Stephen W. Ritterbush, of Arthur D. Little Program Systems Management Company, assesses the risks associated with the financial and management aspects of international projects. He stresses the need for improvement in front-end assessment of risks in the emerging international project environment. Chapter 11 reveals some state-of-the-art thinking on the needs of owner-management in monitoring and controlling large projects. I discuss the new role of owners in the project-management process, pointing out that the most important organizational factor in the 1980s may be the continuing upward shift of responsibility for projects from constructors to owners and financiers. Chapter 12 assesses the information-technology tools available for large, complex projects. Ivars Avots, of Arthur D. Little Program Systems Management Company, surveys the current automation aids with respect to the special needs of projects involving widely separated, remote locations and requiring multiple levels of management-control information. Chapter 13 closes part IV with a penetrating examination of major risk factors in giant projects. Allen Sykes, group financial director of Willis Faber, Ltd., London, identifies and discusses some of the commonly neglected risks and presents the way to avoid disaster in dealing with the problem.

Part V, the final section of the book, is titled "Organizing and Managing Human Resources." It addresses the issues of structuring projects and dealing with personnel resources in the new project environment of the 1980s. Chapter 14 discusses the very important considerations of organizing to deal adequately with change. Peter W.G. Morris, of the Arthur D. Little Programs Systems Management Company Cairo office, provides a detailed assessment of the factors associated with structuring to accommodate the needs of large-scale, dynamic projects. In chapter 15, David I. Cleland, professor of engineering management at the University of Pittsburgh, concludes with a discussion of some of the human considerations in project management. He points out the changes that occur in an organization's existing culture with the introduction of project management and refers to the resulting cultural ambience that ultimately emerges.

Acknowledgments

I would like to express a word of appreciation to the contributing authors who made this book possible. In addition, my special thanks go to Dennis Smith, of the Arthur D. Little Program Systems Management Company consulting staff, who played a major role in coordinating and facilitating the publication of this book.

**Part I
Introduction and Overview**

1

Management Challenges in the 1980s: What Is Ahead in Project Management

John F. Magee

Project management is now a specific management discipline, albeit a relatively young one, having evolved over the past twenty years. It started within the federal government—principally the Department of Defense and the National Aeronautics and Space Administration (NASA). The spectacular success these agencies had with project management in the 1950s and 1960s, plus the growing recognition that this management approach is essential to accomplish most large, complex, unique tasks, led to rapid extension of project-management applications outside the defense-aerospace community. Now, however, the appropriateness of project-management methods to all sizes of projects, in a wide range of situations and a variety of organizations, has been generally accepted by industries, governments, and institutions all over the world.

The experience gained thus far in applying the discipline of project management has contributed to the development of a formal set of principles and practices that can be taught in an educational format and thus can be passed along as a vital element of practical management theory. Evidence can be found in the flourishing educational programs in project management that are available today. Institutions of higher learning are now offering project-management courses at the undergraduate and graduate levels, while a variety of seminars and short courses are conducted throughout the country each year. Industrial and construction firms are adding training programs to indoctrinate managers and staff members in project-management tools and techniques that are tailored to their particular needs.

Another evidence of the rise in influence of project management is the gradual transfer of project-management principles, in the form of matrix management, to the more permanent management institutions within firms. Matrix-management concepts were developed to their highest degree over the past several years within project-management environments. We are now finding that many of these matrix-management principles can be applied to the organizational interfaces within permanently structured, non-project-oriented organizations.

Although project management has come of age as a discipline in its own

3

right, it is still evolving through definition and refinement. Many of the tools and techniques of project management will undergo drastic changes in the next decade. The new capabilities made available through emerging computer technology will allow processing speeds, capacities, and graphic innovations of considerable importance to project-planning and control functions. In addition, the application of minicomputers, distributed processing, and interactive data-processing and communication networks can further revolutionize project managers' methods of generating and distributing management information. The assimilation and application of new technology and methods in project management will present a notable challenge during the 1980s.

The refinement of project management as a discipline is not confined, however, to practitioners and the effects of technological change. It is being gradually defined by the results of litigation as well as by wide-reaching legislation and executive orders at local, state, and federal government levels. Regulatory, socioeconomic, and similar external factors are shaping the body of project-management practice, particularly in the realm of the very large and complex projects.

Finally, the period of the 1980s is ushering in a trend of one-of-a-kind superprojects, which are so different from one another that no learning factor or experience curve can yet be applied to them. Although unique superprojects have been undertaken throughout history, the nature and cost of many of the current projects present project planners and managers with unforeseen challenges. Prospects are strong for growing numbers of very large projects, using more sophisticated technology, involving more complex organizational forms, having greater interface and involvement with public interests, and often being built in remote, hard-to-support locations.

This upswing in the number of large projects involving sophisticated concepts and highly demanding conditions, often international in scope, poses the greatest challenge to project-management disciplines, tools, and techniques for the 1980s. Fortunately, innovative developments in project management offer managers the promise of new state-of-the-art approaches to dealing effectively with these challenges. The following chapters will address this subject by examining some of the key project-management problems facing us in the 1980s and how these challenges might be met.

2 The New Project Environment

Albert J. Kelley

The complex project environment in the 1980s—technical, environmental and sociopolitical—will raise new management issues and problems. To deal with these problems, a new breed of manager must evolve.

The understanding many people now have of project management really involves only the implementation phase. As projects become more complex, however, the implementation phase becomes just one part of a very large task—one that starts off as a concept and must be carried all the way through to a new, functioning entity (see figure 2-1). To cope with the complexities, project managers and their teams will have to plan, plan again, and then plan some more. It is necessary to have good initial baseline planning and continual replanning as the project moves along, since many changes, both expected and unexpected, affect the project as it moves through its various phases. Many organizations have found planning to be the key to project success in meeting new and changing conditions and thus to stability in their operations.

The purpose of any planning process is to define objectives and then define strategy and tactics to achieve these objectives. In a project-planning process, one determines what is to be done, how it is to be done, who will do it, when it will be done, and how much it will cost. Successful planning, however, is or should be, a continuous, iterative process, especially for large, complex projects. In such projects, there often will be a new plan every month, even a new plan every week, as the project progresses—not just as a result of slippages or delays, but because new information is being acquired as the project moves ahead. Planning should not be so locked in or so rigid that the project cannot absorb or take advantage of new information as it moves along. In this new environment, planning must provide feedback points for new information and the flexibility to assimilate and act on it.

Thus, planning large, complex projects cannot be simple. It should include a strategic phase followed by a tactical base. Strategic planning on large projects is analogous to strategic planning in a corporation. The project group must decide basically what it wants to do and what strategies are necessary to achieve its goals. The strategic-planning phase, however, is often rushed through, neglected, or even bypassed in the rush to proceed to

5

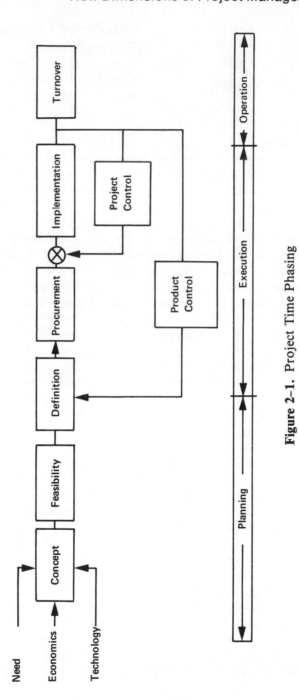

Figure 2–1. Project Time Phasing

the tactical-planning phase. In recognition of the importance of strategic planning, procedures and techniques analogous to corporate strategic planning, such as profiling, have been developed that are applicable to individual projects or classes of projects by either owner or constructor-manufacturer organizations. In tactical planning, the project group must define how it is going to accomplish the project and must schedule it month by month and week by week.

In general, the planning, management, and organization of a major project are somewhat similar to such activities in a corporation, but in many ways they are very different.

Management of Transient versus Steady-State Phenomena

In comparing the mangement of a corporation to that of a project, one can make an analogy to engineering practice. In engineering practice, we have steady-state phenomena and transient phenomena. Each of these is handled by well-known, defined mathematical tools, but each has different ground rules and different impacts on the overall system.

In the normal business operations of a corporation, management is monitoring a gradually changing situation and trying to maintain stability or, it is hoped, even achieve some growth. This growth, however, is gradual compared to that expected in a project, where the increase in manpower and expenditure of money builds to a peak and then levels or drops off. Looking at the familiar cumulative S-curve of project resources and the rate curve of the same function (see figure 2-2), we can draw some interesting analogies. The rate curve looks very much like an impulse function, and the cumulative S-curve looks like a step function.

Transient phenomena are what the project manager is trying to manage. A project is, in fact, the transient step function or perturbation that appears on the scene, changes or adds something, and departs. The project team is trying to get a job done, get out, and leave something new and different behind. Thus in project management we have a very dynamic as well as complex function to manage. Project management's job is to plan for that function and implement it, including development of a tracking and control system that will permit a high degree of sensible management in a fast-moving atmosphere.

Project and institutional management have also been characterized as nonlinear and linear management (see figure 2-3). There are many nonlinearities in a project, whereas, in an institutional setting, once the institution is established, phenomena are generally linear. New-product introduction, however, has many elements similar to project management and has benefited from project-management techniques.

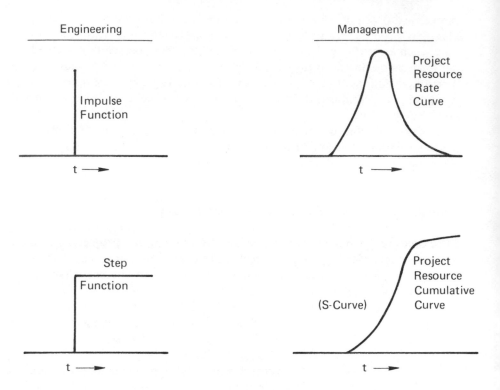

Figure 2–2. Transient Phenomena

In project planning and management, a project manager is really achieving not equilibrium but disequilibrium. A project manager is trying to plan and manage a situation that, by definition, is never in equilibrium, never settles down, and is different every day. As soon as the project gets to the top of the rate curve, it has to go down again.

Because people are trying to do themselves out of jobs by careful project planning, psychological problems are involved. The faster they get a job done, the faster they are out of a job. Thus, they do not have the same incentives as they do in longer-range, stable situations.

Management of Unknown Phenomena

In the 1980s, project managers will have to find solutions to the many stumbling blocks encountered in the management of very large projects—that is, the superprojects that have become prominent during the last two decades.

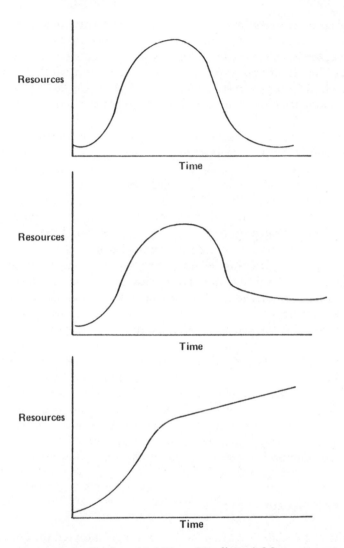

Figure 2-3. Project (Ad Hoc, Nonlinear) Management

Superprojects are much less comprehensible than small projects. Program evaluation and review techniques (PERT) can give us a grasp of small, medium, and some large projects; in superprojects, however, a significant project undertaking is merely a branch of a larger network. If, as is often done, PERT diagrams are drawn in the same scale for superprojects as for smaller projects, the networks are so complex that we do not understand how to use them.

Very large projects involve numerous unknowns; thus, the project's management usually has much to learn as the project progresses. The bigger the project, the less clear are the details. A project manager of large projects must have the vision and tools to see the project as a whole, rather than worrying about comparatively minor details. Thus, the large-project manager has to manage more remotely, through other people and through directives.

Model building and analogs of small projects, which can be done with some degree of success these days, may not be of great value on large projects, because many of the linkages may not be fully understandable and some of the assumptions may not be valid. Several years ago, the American Academy of the Advancement of Science (AAAS) studied several historical project-management situations, one involving the building of large railways across the United States. In that study, the AAAS found that the manager of one of the major links across the country, who had been a successful manager of the Erie Railway in New York, said that the construction and operation of a small railroad bore no relation to the construction and management of a large railroad, such as he was trying to build across the country. There were no set situations; he had to learn as he went along. Obviously, experience helps, but one cannot assume that a large project is merely a group of small projects put together.

The paradox in these situations is that the larger and more complex a project, the greater need there is for better planning early, when the information on which the plan must be based is less certain. As a result, in the planning stage, we often shy away from or postpone many of the decisions that are needed. If we have never been there before, it is human nature to back off and say it is too difficult to make the decisions. An educated guess or informed opinion is better than one might think, however.

Managing the System

During the last decade, we often have unwittingly adopted the concept that the system is the solution. Anyone who has been involved in project management for any length of time has heard many times, particularly from clients, "Give me a computerized PERT-type project control system that I can quickly install and use." That approach leaves out a few things, however, such as the work packages and their organization and management, which may not even be compatible with the specific computerized control system. In this complex world, the system as the solution may neglect information requirements for different people at different responsibility levels. The larger the project, the more levels in the hierarchy become involved and need information. Various types of information are needed for execution contractors, for field supervisors, for the project manager and his staff, for the owner, and for the financiers of the project. The larger the project, the more different the needs, and thus the more custom tailoring it will require.

A successful project manager on a large, complex project usually identifies the controlling variables during the project-planning process. Often despite complex networks, work-breakdown structures (figure 2–4), and computers, he gets to the heart of the matter and finds the key variables that he, as project manager, can use to measure and control. These may or may not be variables that emerge from a standard control system. The project manager and his team must determine for themselves those variables that are different for particularly new and innovative projects. An experienced project manager will probably have two or three ways of getting this information, with different cross-checks. He will not depend entirely on a mechanized system but will have inputs from his own communication network, whether it be formal or informal.

In the new project environment of the 1980s, one must avoid the 1970s management approach of getting fancier and fancier—always looking for a control system to provide automatic management. This approach may be attributed to the fact that most project managers and their immediate staffs have come up through technical or engineering professions, in which everything must be quantified. Thus, some seek the right equation or the right computer program by which the problem can be made to solve itself automatically.

Why should one expect automatic management in projects in very complex dynamic situations? It is not expected and not looked for in a stable corporate environment. Corporations do not look for automatic management; they look for any tool they can use. Few managers running corporations expect a computer or an automatic control system to run their company. Paradoxically, however, in the more volatile, unstable management environment of projects, many project groups continue to search for the system that is the solution.

As projects get larger and more complex, we are beginning to back away from overquantified approaches and to look more at organizational factors. In the large-project environment, people become more important. Larger projects are more labor-intensive. Because there are more people, we must delegate more, and we must manage people better. Thus, in dealings with labor unions, there are productivity as well as labor-agreement considerations. With larger, more complex projects, the project manager and his staff, who have always been the key figures, acquire much more responsibility: they must be innovative; they must be entrepreneurial; and they must be leaders.

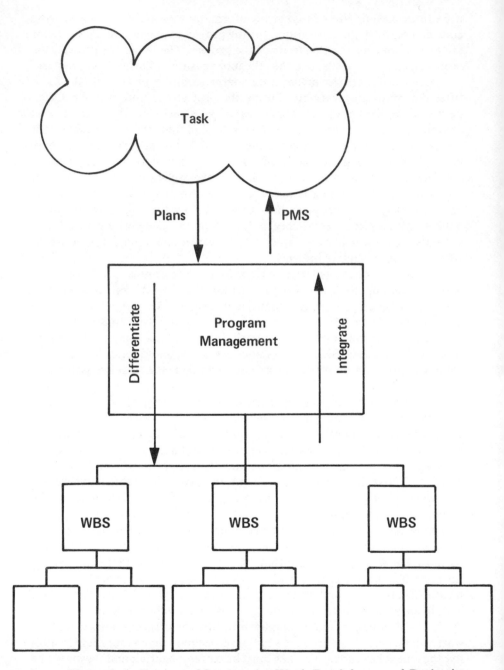

Figure 2-4. Program-Management Work Breakdown and Packaging

Providing Project Maneuverability and Stability

As projects become larger and more complex, the project organization must adapt to more new events and conditions. To do this, it must acquire maneuverability, but this usually means giving up some stability. A good analogy would be the Wright brothers' first airplane. Many had tried to fly before by making a stable airplane—one that would fly hands-off—and they had failed. The Wright brothers, however, gave up some stability—roll stability—for ease of turning or maneuverability, an approach that has carried through to current conventional aircraft; if the controls are let go, the plane will roll over into an unstable spiral. Thus, when the Wright brothers destabilized the airplane, they acquired maneuverability and flyability.

In a sense, this is what we should reach for in new project organizations—giving up some stability for maneuverability and adaptability. We must be fluid in our thinking, not letting organization charts rule the project. We must be able to regroup large numbers of people and quickly define authority and responsibility to meet new situations. Thus, the so-called dotted-line relationships in project organizations can be just as important as the solid-line relationships on the organizational chart—even more important for larger projects. These dotted-line relationships more often than not cannot be written down; they are cohort or working relationships, often developed through task-responsibility matrices. Thus, they must be developed properly and identified and encouraged wherever possible, since they establish important communication links as well as working relationships.

Assuming New Responsibilities

Perhaps the most important organizational factor in the 1980s will be the new and increasing shift of responsibility upward from constructors to owners and financiers, all of whom affect organization-control systems and reporting systems. This upward shift of responsibility results from the shift of risk. The owner will have to take on more project responsibility, even though he usually is not prepared to do so, since he is not a project manager. He must and will do something, however, to be better able to manage his new risk environment.

Social, political, and environmental factors are becoming increasingly important as projects become larger. We are familiar with the ecological factors; political factors are also significant; and legal, regulatory, and public-reaction factors are increasingly important. Evidence of such influence is seen in the proliferation of government regulations. The unwillingness of

the public to endorse new projects and the litigious nature of society substantially increase project-liability risks in even the most routine operations.
All these factors must be taken into consideration in the planning and management of a project. The larger the project, the more turbulent will be the
impact on the environment. In fact, the project may change the environment. As an example, many in the western United States are concerned
about the plans for deployment of the MX missile system. They contend
that the MX missile will change their entire environment.

A project manager must identify the external factors, such as regulations, early in the planning stage and must be constantly aware of external
pressures from government agencies to the public and the financial community, all of which are generally transferred to the project. He also must take
into account the fact that inflation not only increases the overall cost of the
project but also affects internal economic trade-offs. If the project manager
has not identified external factors early and tracked them accurately, they
may replace the controlling variables on which his project plans were based.

In defense projects and other areas, the management of software development presents a formidable challenge. Many of the management techniques used for hardware projects are inadequate, and sophisticated techniques for software management have not yet evolved.

In the new project environment, the financing and financial management of projects in an inflationary economy will deserve priority attention.
The project manager and his team will find themselves managing and controlling costs throughout the entire financial cycle of a project, starting with
the development of the initial financial package.

Project executives of the next decade will have less time to adapt to
change, and they will be subject to greater penalties for their mistakes. To
react quickly and effectively, they will need a combination of technical,
business, and sociological expertise and exposure to a wide variety of disciplines. They will have to work well with others to be good managers, in the
sense that management is the art of getting things done through other people.

Part II
Policy and Environment

3

Managing Multi-Organization Enterprises: The Emerging Strategic Frontier

Mel Horwitch and
C.K. Prahalad

A new kind of institution, the Multi-Organization Enterprise (MOE) is increasingly being used to respond to large-scale societal concerns. The MOE is generally a collaboration of organizations in government, industry, and other sectors. This collaboration is created to meet visible, large-scale, often technologically based needs that are usually beyond the technical, financial, political, and managerial capabilities of any single organization.[1]

MOEs generally exhibit the following major characteristics:

1. They are usually established to accomplish a mission that may be as focused as landing a person on the moon or as broad as implementing a national energy plan.
2. An MOE often contains participating groups that exhibit different cultures, assumptions, priorities, and goals.
3. Both public and private organizations can be parts of an MOE.
4. Usually only a small part of each of the various organizations that participate in an MOE is actually involved in that effort, and the component organizations continue to maintain their separate identities.
5. MOEs are usually large. They require significant funds and employ thousands of employees from several organizations.

MOEs are highly diverse, and their rise is a worldwide phenomenon. They are being established in increasing numbers to deal with such critical issues as energy, transportation, communication/information, aerospace, and economic development. They are found in industrialized nations and developing countries. A representative list might include the following:[2]

Liquid Metal Fast Breeder Reactor program (U.S.);

Super-Phoenix—breeder reactor program (France);

Connecticut Resource (Solid Waste) Recovery Authority (U.S.);

The program to make the Island of Hawaii energy self-sufficient (U.S.);

Various nondefense aerospace programs—e.g., Apollo, Space Shuttle, the Concorde, and Airbus (U.S. and elsewhere);

Various national energy plans, such as those in the U.S., Spain, Iran (under the Shah), and Brazil;

The program to make liquid fuel (gasahol) from sugar cane (Brazil);

The Jubail Industrial Complex (Saudi Arabia);

Development of an iron and steel complex in Nigeria's 1975–1980 Five Year Plan;

EURODIF—a European uranium enrichment project (various countries);

System X communications plan (Britain);

The global rise of MOEs will almost certainly continue and will probably intensify. The tendency to conceptualize problems and issues and to formulate solutions in ways that cross organizational, industrial, geographical, and public-private boundaries has emerged over the last twenty years as a dominant mind-set for policy making and decision making. In part, this development arose because of a growing ability and willingness to view social issues in an interdisciplinary fashion, to model or to simulate complex problems, and to evaluate decisions using holistic analytical techniques like systems analysis. Enterprises are then structured to follow these conceptual approaches.

During the decade-and-a-half following World War II, the greatest MOE activity was in national defense, where MOEs were established primarily to develop weapon systems. Since then the management lessons learned from this military experience, under the rubric of "project management," have been advocated for nonmilitary missions.[3]

The transfer of military-spawned project management techniques to civilian purposes, however, was never really successful. Weapon systems programs in the 1950s and early 1960s possessed certain attributes that allowed military project management techniques to be effective. These defense MOEs usually had a protective national defense cloak that frequently helped to shield them from outside criticism and scrutiny. Moreover, although private contractors were heavily involved in research, development, and construction, the ultimate customer for these MOEs was the government. The function of the end product was primary noneconomic. Consequently, pure economic profitability and return-on-investment evaluation methods were usually inappropriate for military MOEs. Finally, the relevant environment until the mid-1960s was essentially benign. There was a tendency to accept the need for national defense projects and to defer to the opinions of defense experts. In sum, until the mid-1960's, MOEs were largely military in character, and they existed in a contained and friendly world.

The Apollo program, although nonmilitary, also possessed many of the features of military MOEs. Apollo, too, was a creature of the Cold War; it had no direct economic end use; the government was the final customer. Apollo also possessed a protective cloak in the form of an absolute presidential commitment. It involved the same industries that were active in defense MOEs; the decision-making network was also fairly favorable and containable. Consequently, many military project management approaches were successfully transferred and refined for use in this space project in the 1960s.

But during the 1960s and 1970s the domain of MOE activity grew and diversified. A new class of MOEs has emerged. This new group operates in highly controversial areas, such as transportation, energy, economic development, civilian aerospace, and communication/information. Containment for long periods of time, practiced successfully my managers of earlier weapon systems programs and Apollo, has become increasingly difficult to accomplish. These MOEs generally have a different and fuller relationship with the private sector. In addition to private firms' involvement in research, development, and construction, end products more often than not are supposed to be adopted by commercial firms for manufacture and distribution. Consequently, the relationship between the government's top manager of an MOE and the private sector has become more complex. Not only does the government select and monitor its contractors in developing a project, but increasingly the government also has to sell its project to potential private backers and users.

The appearance and increasing importance of civilian-oriented MOEs severely complicate the task of successfully managing such endeavors. The traditional MOE protective cloak (under the name of national defense, national prestige, or absolute presidential commitment) that tended to help buffer former military- and space-oriented MOEs from criticism has lost much of its effectiveness. The opportunities for intervention from potential opponents or skeptics have grown significantly. In addition, with commercialization often as the ultimate goal, the influence of economic return-on-investment and profitability analyses and evaluations has increased.

By the end of the 1960s, the socio-political context had changed. Outsiders claiming to represent the general public, and perceiving transcendent public interests in these enterprises, were no longer willing to defer automatically to experts who backed a particular MOE. This general development and the specific rise of more open MOE systems allowed the growing number of potential interventionists greater opportunities to become involved in MOE decision-making. Moreover, the new participants have become sophisticated operators in the relevant political and bureaucratic environment, and they come armed with their own experts and data. The balance of power between proponents, opponents, and neutral participants, therefore, now often shifts.

The MOE is now subject to radical transformations in its environment, in its relevant set of stakeholders, or in its organizational structure. Consequently, the ultimate outcome of an MOE has become less predictable. Often at the end of this series of changes, the MOE is aborted or rendered ineffective. In particular MOEs, after having been elegantly designed, carefully structured, and aggressively promoted, often flounder on the shoals of implementation and management. In sum, few MOEs can be considered outright successes, in spite of their growing number. More fail, and for even more the outcome is still unknown.

This changed MOE environment and the enlarged and expanded set of MOE missions raise new concerns for improving MOE managerial effectiveness and strategy making. Moreover, because key MOE management requirements are distinct from those for private multi-business corporations, we cannot rely on private sector administrative know-how.[4] Instead, we must rethink the question of what constitutes the essential factors for effectively devising and implementing an MOE management strategy.

This examination of MOE management strategies is based on a familiarity with several MOEs and on an in-depth analysis of four diverse nonmilitary MOEs—the American SST program, the American effort to develop synthetic fuels from coal, the SITE program (an Indian communications satellite project), and the development of the Universal Product Code and Standard Symbol for the U.S. grocery industry. They were selected because they represent in diverse ways the new wave of MOEs and they illustrate managerial success and managerial failure. Each enterprise will be briefly described, and then the general lessons for MOE management will be discussed.

Four Representative MOEs

The American SST Program

The decade-long American SST program (1961 to 1971) can be viewed as having passed through three important phases.[5] The first phase, termed *containment,* lasted from about 1961 to about mid-1963. It was characterized by a contained and predictable set of participants in industry, in the aerospace-oriented government agencies, and in relevant congressional committees that were favorably disposed towards the project.

Developing an American SST suited the generally optimistic mood of the country. The effort was aided by the creation of the Anglo-French Concorde program in 1962 and by the aggressive prodding of Federal Aviation Administration (FAA) Administrator Najeeb Halaby. Halaby was at the peak of his power on June 5, 1963, when President Kennedy announced at the Air Force Academy that the United States would begin its own SST. But under Kennedy's ground rules, the manufacturers would be required to contribute 25 percent of the total development costs of this estimated $1 billion program, and in no case would the government's contribution exceed $750 million.

From mid-1963 until about 1968, the SST program went through a *fragmentation* phase. During this period, the SST program was increasingly battered by numerous problems: bureaucratic jealousies, economic doubt, lack of managerial confidence, changing loci of policy-making power, technical uncertainty, changing and ambiguous presidential support, a growing number of actors, the beginnings of criticism in the media, and the emergence of organized public opposition. The fabric that held the SST program together was ripped apart. Important fragments of the SST program eventually settled in a variety of organizations and interested groups.

Under the pressure of industry complaints about the cost-sharing guidelines and of general doubts about the FAA's managerial ability, President Johnson created in April 1964 an all-powerful, high-level President's Advisory Committee on Supersonic Transport (PAC) with Defense Secretary Robert S. McNamara as chairman. McNamara quickly supplanted Halaby as the most powerful actor in the SST program. He forced successive delays in the SST design-selection competition. His demands also resulted in conflicting SST economic analyses being performed by at least three agencies and in sonic boom test responsibility being shared by three public or quasi-public institutions. Halaby left office in early July 1965. His successor as FAA Administrator was an air force general, and another air force general was named director of the SST program. Both individuals were experienced project managers, and they attempted to regain control of the SST program for the FAA. But severe technical problems with the winning swing-wing design by Boeing (selected at the end of 1966) led to a two-year delay before Boeing resubmitted a new and acceptable fixed-wing aircraft.

Meanwhile, in 1966 serious press criticism began to appear, and just as significant, effective and organized anti-SST opposition soon emerged. Dr. William Shurcliff, a physicist at the Harvard University Linear Accelerator, formed the Citizens League Against the Sonic Boom in March 1967. Shurcliff initiated an intensive letter-writing and advertising campaign, and he protested pro-SST official reports.

In September 1969, President Nixon ignited the third phase of the SST program, *explosion,* by announcing a $96 million fiscal 1970 request to construct two SST prototypes. In April 1970, Nixon appointed William M. Magruder as new SST director. Magruder, an engineer and a former test pilot, had been second in command of Lockheed's ill-starred SST effort. Nixon's go-ahead decision triggered unprecedented protest from national environmental groups. A host of environmental organizations created a national Coalition against the SST, and the important focus of SST activity shifted away from its bureaucratic base to Capitol Hill and to national and local opposition groups. SST opposition spread rapidly during the summer and fall of 1970. Studies raising new doubts about the program appeared, and fifteen diverse leading economists announced their opposition. As the anti-SST Coalition marshaled various experts, the SST emerged as a hotly debated senatorial campaign issue, and many state and local anti-SST groups surfaced.

The anti-SST forces prevailed. In early December 1970, the Senate passed an amendment to delete all SST funds from the Department of Transportation Appropriations Bill, and the following March both the House and the Senate voted against SST funding. The SST program was soon terminated.

The American Effort to Develop Synthetic Fuels
from Coal

Like the SST program, the American effort to develop coal-based synthetic fuels grew both in complexity and in number of participants.[6] But unlike the SST program, the synthetic fuels effort had always been unfocused, and its ultimate outcome has yet to be decided.

The first period, which lasted from the end of World War II to the mid-1950s, was one of *significant activity.* Under pressure of wartime and a subsequent oil shortage during the winter of 1948, the government funded a relatively large synfuels R&D effort, and there was even an attempt in the late 1940s to launch an $8 billion crash program. However, with the increasing availability of cheap foreign crude, the adamant opposition of the oil industry, and the weakening of liberal activism, the first synfuels program vanished.

The advocates of coal-based synfuels (including coal industry executives, coal region members of Congress, and like-minded bureaucrats) attempted to regroup, and synfuels entered their second phase, a *long hiatus,* which began in the mid-1950s and lasted until the early 1970s. These advocates sought a powerful and enthusiastic agency along the lines of the Atomic Energy Commission which was effectively promoting coal's new competitor in the utility sector—nuclear energy. But the coal supporters won only a small unit in the Department of Interior, the Office of Coal Research (OCR), established in the early 1960s. OCR's staff was small, its bureaucratic clout modest, and its funding limited. Still, its activities had some impact. OCR signed a number of contracts for various gasification and liquefaction projects during the 1960s. These activities brought forth a number of optimistic public comments on the prospects of synthetic fuels by OCR contractors and officials.

This flurry of public enthusiam over liquefaction and gasification had at least one other important effect: it served as a powerful magnet for pulling oil firms and, to a lesser extent, gas firms into the coal industry. In the mid- and late 1960s and early 1970s, Exxon, Texaco, Continental Oil, Occidental, Sun Oil, Columbia Gas, El Paso Natural Gas, Texas Eastern Transmission, and other oil and gas firms acquired coal reserves or companies, established internal synfuels research units, or entered into joint synfuels consortia. By the late 1960s and early 1970s, such firms found it hard to resist the temptation to see coal as a potential synfuel feedstock for their refineries, pipelines, or petrochemical plants.

The third phase of the U.S. synthetic fuels effort, termed *premature expansion,* began in the early 1970s and lasted until mid-1979. The involvement of oil and gas firms continued to grow in synfuels R&D, and sparked by the 1973–74 oil embargo and the resulting energy crisis, government synfuels funding also increased substantially. However, although serious attempts were made to design and implement relatively large gasification and liquefaction projects, by the end of this phase, practically all such large-scale projects had been significant delayed, stalled, aborted, or abandoned. The Wesco and Conpaso gasification projects in New Mexico and the Coalcon clean-boiler-fuel project in Illinois were examples of such endeavors. All three of these ambitious joint ventures ultimately were not constructed during the 1970s due to a combination of technical, economic, environmental, political, and managerial factors.

The U.S. synfuels effort has recently entered its fourth phase, *uncertain takeoff.* The government in 1978 and early 1979 had apparently turned away from synfuels in favor of stressing R&D for improving the direct combustion of coal. But in response primarily to the Iranian crisis and the resulting gas lines in mid-1979, a sudden new emphasis in synfuels surged first on Capitol Hill and then in the White House. On June 30, 1980, a public Synthetic Fuels Corporation was signed into law to provide loans, loan guarantees, and price guarantees; to enter joint ventures; and to operate a limited number of government-owned plants in a two-phase, twelve-year synfuels program, totaling potentially $88 billion.[7]

The outcome of this current phase is unclear. A vigorous and viable synthetic fuels industry may be emerging, or in the face of new disappointments (like the SST), a new wave of protest and backlash may again limit synfuels as a feasible energy alternative.

Satellite Instructional Television Experiment

Unlike the SST or (thus far) synthetic fuels, the Satellite Instructional Television Experiment (SITE) program in India can be considered a managerial success.[8] Its basic goals were achieved. SITE's general objectives included:

> Gaining experience in the development, testing, and management of a satellite-based instructional television system, particularly for rural areas:

> Emphasizing program content in the areas of family planning, agricultural practices, national integration values, adult education, teaching training, occupational skills, and health and hygiene;

> Demonstrating the potential value of satellite broadcast TV in the practical instruction of village inhabitants;

> Stimulating overall national development in India.

In 1962 the Indian Department of Atomic Energy (DAE), under the leadership of Dr. Vikram Sarabhai, established the Indian National Committee for Space Research, and throughout the early 1960s Sarabhai and his organization promoted the notion of a satellite-based communications system for India. Sarabhai, a member of a wealthy family, a close associate of Prime Minister Nehru, and on friendly terms with top decision makers throughout the world, was the ideal champion. Largely through his efforts, DAE with U.S. support established an experimental satellite communications earth station at Ahmedabad, India in 1967. Four years later using Indian engineers trained in the Ahmedabad project. India built its first commercial earth station in Bombay. Meanwhile in 1966, Sarabhai spearheaded a feasibility study on Indian satellite communications, and the following year a UNESCO-sponsored study project on the same subject also began. In 1968 Sarabhai became chairman of a new Indian interministerial study group on satellite communication. In September 1969 following the recommendations of a joint DAE-NASA team, DAE and NASA signed a formal agreement to cooperate in developing an American-Indian satellite TV project, which eventually became SITE. NASA was to focus on the satellite, and various Indian organizations were to be responsible for all ground support equipment and software program development. DAE coordinated contact with NASA and with other contractors who were performing feasibility studies. Sarabhai chaired most of the committees and provided momentum for the project. He used his close personal relationships with high-level officials frequently and effectively. He successfully maintained a broad base of support and also improved Indian competencies by sponsoring more specialized units relating to SITE in DAE, in other governmental agencies, and in various ad hoc interagency bodies.

Although Sarabhai died at the end of 1971, he had been able to generate a momentum that carried SITE to a successful completion. Between 1973 and 1975, a period of *intense activity,* numerous organizational interfaces were coordinated, and the complex technical tasks required for SITE were accomplished. For an entire year in 1975, remote receivers in 2,400 villages, grouped in six clusters, received TV programs transmitted by satellite. In addition to demonstrating that extremely advanced technologies like satellite-based communication can be developed by and implemented in developing countries, SITE showed that complex MOES can be managed successfully.

As the SITE program was winding down its year-long experiment in 1976, a host of federal agencies began activity to seek to gain control of the new enterprise and *share the spoils.* With Sarabhai gone, DAE no longer possessed overall power, and a variety of agencies (including India's space agency, post office, and broadcasting ministry) began to contend for organizational leadership in the satellite communications field.

The Development of Universal Product Code
and Standard Symbol for the U.S. Grocery Industry

The development of the Universal Product Code (UPC) and the Standard Symbol for the U.S. grocery industry is also considered an MOE even though it took place mostly in the private sector.[9] Like other MOEs, the development of this technology was an extremely complex and multi-party process that involved a large number of technologically difficult tasks and a wide variety of organizations. But this MOE is unlike the others already described, because from the very beginning, its products had to meet rigid economic feasibility standards that were directly imposed by private sector firms. It is also different because it encompassed a dual set of similar phases: one set for the UPC and one for the Standard Symbol. Each set exhibited the same three-phase pattern: an initial phase of *gaining commitment,* followed by or concurrent with a period of *detailed techno-economic analyses,* and ending with a phase of *decision making and selection.* This MOE was successful in so far as there was widespread industry acceptance of the chosen code and symbol. But actual implementation has been slower than anticipated.

In the late 1960s as the retail segment of the U.S. grocery industry began to suffer a cost-price squeeze, interest in attempts to increase productivity grew. With labor accounting for about 50 percent of all store expenses and with front-end labor 40 percent of all labor expenses in a store, about 20 percent of all store expenses were attributable to one clearly identifiable step in store operations— the front-end check-out function. Starting in the mid-1960's, scattered efforts were made to stimulate store automation. But the real beginning of innovation in this area took place in the summer of 1970, when leaders of the various trade groups representing the industry created an ad hoc committee to study the feasibility of a Universal Product Code (UPC) for the industry. The committee was chaired by the president of H.J. Heinz Company, and its members included representatives of all sectors of the grocery industry, including manufacturers, distributors, wholesalers, and retailers. At its first meeting, the committee retained McKinsey and Company, a management consulting firm, for the staff work. The committee, with McKinsey's help, carefully and comprehensively evaluated the UPC, focusing on the retailing part of the operation (even though the UPC was potentially attractive for other elements of the grocery chain, such as inventory management). The evaluation used cost-benefit analysis and considered a host of critical noneconomic factors, including the adequacy of consumer price information and the possible involvement of the Federal Trade Commission (FTC). (All members of the committee agreed to make no public statement until the UPC had been cleared by the FTC.)

In order to gain the commitment of the entire complex industry, the committee contacted a critical mass of firms and trade groups and then explained the UPC. Between March and May 1971, committee members and consultants made over 250 presentations. This immense effort was successful. The committee received wide industry support for the UPC, and a decision to adopt the UPC was announced in May 1971.

At this time, the committee appointed a subcommittee to choose a Standard Symbol. The subcommittee was given about $1 million, collected from the industry, to work on the problem, and the president of First National Stores was appointed subcommittee chairman. From May to December 1971, the subcommittee worked to develop appropriate guidelines in order to establish a framework for its own internal operations and for managing its relations with equipment vendors, printers, government agencies, consumer groups, trade associations, and a host of other interested parties. In order to communicate to all interested groups, the subcommittee issued several statements and manuals outlining all of the diverse aspects of its decision-making procedures.

The actual data collection and detailed analysis phase for the symbol took place between January 1972 and March 1973. A test store was established to evaluate the feasibility of an automatic check-out and to monitor customer reaction, and the test results were widely disseminated. The economics of source printing the symbols was also examined in great detail. Several firms proposed design formats for the symbol, and each alternative was evaluated in detail. The subcommittee depended heavily on outside staff work and expertise. McKinsey consultants coordinated the active work of the subcommittee, and experts from the Battelle Memorial Institute, M.I.T., equipment manufacturers, and printers were consulted frequently.

This in-depth evaluation produced a radical shift in design philosophy. Originally RCA with its circular "bull's-eye" symbol had an inside track. However, after listening to proposals from IBM and others, the subcommittee concluded that a rectangular bar design was more robust in terms of printing, and ultimately the rectangular bar symbol was selected in the spring of 1973.

The subcommittee's Standard Symbol work was at least a partial success. Within three years of the announcement, more than 75 percent of all grocery items carried the symbol. But the subcommittee and the industry had overlooked the impact of consumer activism and opposition to the elimination of price marking on individual items. Also underestimated were the operational and financial problems facing stores in their move to an automated check-out system.

Devising Effective Strategies for Managing MOEs

The four different patterns of MOE evolution that have been described illustrate the great diversity and complexity of this kind of institution (see table 3-1). Moreover, the existence of different patterns of failure, such as those for the American SST program and the American attempt thus far to develop synthetic fuels from coal, points to the extremely hazardous position in which MOE top managers now find themselves. Yet the existence of comparatively successful patterns, such as those for SITE and the UPC Standard Symbol, shows that, given the appropriate context and strategy, civilian-oriented MOEs can be successfully managed.

Recognize the MOE's Inherent Instability

The first step in achieving a successful long-run MOE management strategy is for top managers to recognize from the beginning the MOE's inherent instability. The potential for radical transformations of an MOE is difficult to discern before such changes actually occur. Forecasting accurately the evolution of an MOE is extremely problematic. Moreover, even if the MOE

Table 3–1
Four MOE Evolutionary Patterns

"Failures"		"Successes"		
American SST Program		**SITE**		
Containment	1961–1963	Commitment	1963–1972	
Fragmentation	1963–1968	Intense activity	1972–1975	
Explosion	1969–1971	Share the spoils	1976–	
American Coal-based		**U.S. Grocery Industry**		
Synfuels				
			UPC	**Standard Symbol**
Significant activity: first				
synfuels program	1944–1955	Gain commitment	1970–May 1971	May–Dec. 1971
		Detailed economic		Jan. 1972–
Long hiatus	1955–1973	analyses	1970–May 1971	Mar. 1973
Premature		Decision making		
expansion	1973–1979	and selection	May 1971	Spring 1973
Uncertain takeoff	1979–			

manager knew the direction of an MOE's change, that manager must be able to select from a complex set of managerial techniques in order to guide the enterprise through a particularly turbulent period. Even so, the manager may devise an inappropriate strategy or may recognize the danger too late to respond meaningfully.

To cope with the MOE's inherent instability, the top MOE manager must devise a strategy that has at least three different dimensions: a process for monitoring and providing feedback from the external environment, a relevant perspective or set of attitudes by the top management group, and an appropriate internal organizational structure.

Track and Assess Early Warning Signals

The top MOE manager must explicitly establish procedures for tracking and assessing early warning signals. Although the MOE's transformations may appear sudden and radical, generalizable evolutionary patterns usually exist, and early indicators of major problem areas frequently surface only to remain unrecognized. There were a number of such signals in the early and middle stages of the SST program, including the following: a significant percentage of negative respondents in early sonic boom tests, the initial controversies over government-industry cost sharing, the consistent criticism of the FAA's managerial capability, the creation of the President's Advisory Committee under McNamara, the formation of Shurcliff's Citizens League against the Sonic Boom, and the general lack of enthusiasm for the program in key parts of the administration. Significantly, many of the unrecognized signals were nontechnical and noneconomic in character. Such indicators should have triggered a significant review of the program. But this did not occur. One cause for this inaction was that a tracking-and-review procedure was not in place, either formally or informally.

In contrast, both in developing the Universal Product Code and Standard Symbol and in SITE, the relevant external environment was carefully monitored. The various impacts of changes in technology, politics, economics, public bureaucracy, and management were taken into account in developing management strategies. In developing the Standard Symbol, a test store was established to evaluate the impact of the symbol on customers. The results of this test, along with findings of several detailed studies, were an important part of the subcommittee's subsequent, impressive symbol-design selection process. Even so, the subcommittee failed to anticipate the strength of consumer activist opposition to the new system. In SITE, a special TV program studio at Ahmedabad was established under the Indian Space Research Organization, even though All-India Radio was responsible for the bulk of the country's television programming. SITE, therefore, had its own capability to develop programs and to conduct its own program evaluation.

As already mentioned, earlier military MOEs had the benefit of a national defense shield to support their existence. The monitoring of a civilian MOE's external environment may help to create an effective cloak. In contrast to the ineffective national prestige argument resorted to frequently by SST advocates, the same national security theme is being used with some success today to buffer a new massive synfuels effort from a variety of outside attacks. Similarly, Sarabhai used the need for national economic development and unity as a shield to protect SITE. Both current synfuels and past SITE advocates, effectively understanding the outside environment, had developed cloaks that successfully matched the mood of the times.

Key Ingredients for MOE Success Are Not Limited
to Technology or Economics

The four MOEs also demonstrate the need for an appropriate managerial perspective and set of attitudes. Perhaps most important in this regard, the MOE top manager must realize that the key ingredients for an MOE's success are by no means limited to technological or economic concerns.

The importance of recognizing the key nontechnical and noneconomic factors is seen in the contrasting examples of SITE and SST. In SITE, Sarabhai could transcend his technical role to deal skillfully with the mangerial, bureaucratic, and political facets of his mission. Successful shepherding of SITE in India was not just a technical task, even though SITE's technical goals were enormously complex and challenging. Managing SITE also required dealing with the interests and concerns of several well-entrenched governmental bureaucracies, including the Ministries of Information and Broadcasting, Posts and Telegraph, Defense, Education, Agriculture, Health and Family Planning, and Atomic Energy. Dangers to SITE lurked everywhere. Some ministries such as Defense or Atomic Energy with sophisticated technical capabilities were potentially attracted to SITE because of its advanced technology. Other ministries such as Education, Agriculture, and Health and Family Planning coveted SITE, because they saw the enterprise operating in their natural jurisdiction. Sarabhai possessed the skill to manage the rivalries between these groups to maintain SITE as a distinct entity and to retain control of the project during its critical phase—the period from 1968 to 1971. He managed to remain in a position to educate all potential participants on how to use the new system in an effective and innovative manner.

In contrast to the leadership of SITE, the SST program leadership had a narrow technocratic and project management prospective during the last half of the 1960s and in 1970. The SST managers and advocates overlooked the massive change that was occurring in American public opinion, which no longer automatically equated technological advance with progress. Social and environmental impacts had also become important. Consequently, the SST managers, stressing national prestige, balance of payments, employments benefits, and technological progress, were not cognizant of the strength of the SST opponents' growing public appeal until it was too late.

A large publicly funded effort like the SST, because it involves so many different groups, always possesses the potential to reflect current or emerging societal views. The importance of nontechnical and noneconomic factors has been supported by other studies. One study pointed to the importance of stability in the external environment, the competence of project management, and society's expectations for the enterprise's rate of growth as crucial determinants of the evolution of MOEs.[10] Another, the Stanford Research Institute's comparative study of eight large-scale projects, concluded that there may be inherent limits and constraints for MOEs due more to organizational/managerial, socio-political, and psychological/motivational factors than to technical and economic ones.[11] Finally, a Rand Corporation analysis of twenty-four federally funded demonstration projects maintained that "political pressure" to demonstrate a premature technology should be resisted and that sufficient slack should be built into the project's schedule to allow for slippage.[12] But clearly, as we have seen in the American SST conflict, the approach suggested by Rand study ignored the ever present potential for sudden uncontrolled transformations, which becomes more likely as programs are delayed or extended.

Recognize the Need to Communicate with and to Understand Diverse Cultures

Accepting the importance of key nontechnical and noneconomic issues is a first step toward recognizing the need to communicate with and to understand the diverse cultures that often significantly affect an MOE at some point. The need to span multiple cultures may not always be apparent. This was true during the long hiatus phase of synthetic fuels, the containment phase of the SST, or any of the three phases of the Universal Product Code and Standard Symbol development. But each of these MOEs in its own way became increasingly complex and visible, and ultimately each involved a much wider variety of interested groups than participated at the beginning of the endeavor. The SST managers never communicated effectively with the increasingly diverse interested parties that significantly affected the program. Even at the end, the last SST program director generally assumed a posture of confrontation and would argue with his adversaries point by point. Until very recently the managers of synthetic fuels efforts were little concerned about outside groups. Synthetic fuels development was simply not a highly visible undertaking. Of course, all that has changed. Synfuels are now perceived to be of high national importance, and they are assuming an increasingly controversial and major role in energy policy. Even the Standard Symbol finally became a target for protest by consumer groups, and now interested parties have prevented this new technological development from realizing its full technical and economic potential.

Include Individuals Representing Various Backgrounds and Views

An important way to maintain an appropriately balanced and diverse perspective is to establish personnel systems and other procedures for bringing into the MOE individuals with varied backgrounds and views. This was accomplished in developing the Universal Product Code and Standard Symbol by extensively using highly diverse committees and outside consultants. At SITE, Sarabhai explicitly recruited a set of individuals, who together represented a portfolio of highly varied work experiences. On the other hand, most of those involved in the SST program had similar technical, bureaucratic, or military backgrounds. It was only in the mid-1960s, for example, after McNamara started receiving negative economic analyses on the SST from other agencies, that the FAA actually created an in-house economic analysis staff group.

The Top Manager Must Be a Project Champion

Ironically, even though the top MOE manager must be careful to see the nontechnical and noneconomic nature of the enterprise, to communicate with diverse groups, and to recognize the danger points in the environment, the top manager must also be an advocate and a champion of the MOE. It is the champion's great desire to see the enterprise completed that provides much of the momentum to overcome obstacles to fruition; to reach out across geographic, organizational, and cultural boundaries to protect and to promote an MOE; and to facilitate overall success. Halaby was such a champion during the containment period of the SST program. His promotional efforts were crucial for successfully starting the effort. Sarabhai was an eminently successful champion for SITE. Similarly, the president of First National Stores (who was chairman of the symbol subcommittee) and the McKinsey consultant (who coordinated the developmental effort) emerged as critical champions in evaluating and selecting the Standard Symbol. On the other hand, where a true and well-positioned champion is lacking (as was the case for synthetic fuels until recently), the likelihood of success for an MOE is small. During the synfuels' long hiatus and premature expansion phases, there were really no clear top managers; instead, there were only scattered coalitions working on separate activities. It is no wonder that such groups or individuals were unable to combat the apathy in the environment and the resulting lack of focus.

We can be even more specific about the ingredients of effective MOE leadership. The MOE champion should possess abilities to communicate effectively with several culturally distant and distinct groups and not be content to be surrounded by people who speak the same language. Sarabhai, in implementing SITE, was able to communicate the political attractiveness of technical issues and vice versa. In the SST case, the political appeal of the program was never effectively made clear.

The MOE champion almost always must motivate people by raising the mission of the MOE beyond selfish personal or departmental ends. At SITE, the mission was interpreted as a national developmental goal and was a source of nationwide inspiration. SITE objectives went beyond those of the original sponsoring agency, DAE. Similarly, the committee and subcommittee structure made the entire grocery industry part of the UPC and Standard Symbol selection process. However, the SST, seen as fulfilling the goals of Halaby and the FAA, basically was viewed as an effort of the FASA and a limited number of relatively predictable proaviation parties.

Finally, the top MOE manager should recognize the legitimacy of dissent and change while focusing on completing the project. Most civilian MOEs will inevitably draw some opposition and will also require change. In successful MOEs dissent and change are often used by their champions. For example, until practically the very last moment, the symbol subcommittee was convinced that the RCA circular symbol was the best choice. But as growing evidence against it surfaced, the subcommittee changed its mind and chose the rectangular bar symbol. In SITE, Sarabhai actually cultivated dissent by contracting for studies by SITE critics so that he could generate new ideas or co-opt potential opposition. In contrast, the SST top managers ignored much of the information that threatened the program and often avoided or ignored those, such as Shurcliff, who raised objections to the project.

Develop an Effective Internal Organizational Structure

The evolutionary pattern of the four MOEs also points to the importance of developing an effective internal organizational structure. Such structures must be sufficiently adaptable to withstand radical transformations and to deal effectively with nontechnical and noneconomic concerns across multiple constituencies. Essentially, top MOE managers must create rather elaborate organizations in the earlier, less complex and more benign phases. In fact, such structures may seem at that early time overorganized, overly complex, and excessive. But the best period to create truly effective MOE organizational systems in the beginning where there is still time to plan and react.

It is easy to understand why devising and implementing an effective strategy for MOEs is so difficult. The heart of a successful MOE strategy is to plan for and expect states that do not yet exist and are difficult to conceive. The concept of strategic "fit" (appraising the strengths and weaknesses of the organizations against the opportunities and threats in the environment) that is so pervasive in the private sector is not appropriate for MOEs Essentially, this is because of the MOE's potential to undergo radical transformations—in other words, extreme and seemingly sudden shifts in the nature of the organization or of its environment. Such transformations can destroy an enterprise, as seen in the SST case. Even leaving the issue of sudden change aside, the traditional concept of strategic fit would be difficult to implement in an MOE context because of the highly complex and changing set of interested parties involved. To attempt to create such a fit would be a time-consuming and ultimately unrewarding exercise. More often than not, certain key factors would be overlooked, and in any case the scene is inherently unstable.

Instead of focusing on fit or on a strategy for dealing with a particular situation at a point in time, the MOE top manager must constantly be looking ahead in order to try paradoxically to anticipate the unexpected. Therefore, effective MOE strategy depends on fluid and adaptive techniques: external monitoring, a flexible and broad perspective, and a complex and sophisticated organizational structure. The MOE manager must somehow combine a legitimate commitment for achieving the MOE's goal with the flexibility and capability to remain one step ahead of failure. The chances for failure are all too real. But the rewards of succeeding for managers and, at time, for society are very great, and at least once in a while an MOE can be managed so that it fulfills at least part of its original promise.

Notes

1. For a review of the current thinking and literature on MOEs, see M. Horwitch, "Designing and Managing Large-Scale Public-Private Technological Enterprises: A State-of-the-Art Review," *Technology in Society* (Autumn 1979):179–182.

2. There are a number of individual case studies on MOEs. They are available through the Intercollegiate Case Clearing House, Soldiers Field Road, Boston, MA 02163. The case studies include:

Managing the U.S. Supersonic Transport Program (A & B), ICH #90678–049–50;

The Tennessee Valley Authority and the Peabody Coal Company, ICH #9–379–038;

TFX: The Commonality Decision, ICG #6–375–035; Voyager and Viking Programs at NASA, ICH #9–375–186;

Background Information on NASA and Planetary and Addendum, ICH #9–375–187–188;

Operation Breakthrough: The Concept and the Record, ICH #9–673–119;

Pacific Light: Wesco, ICH #9–377–899;

Connecticut Resource Recovery Authority, ICH #9–673–123;

McCulloch Oil: Geothermal Energy Project, ICH #9–677–067;

Liquecoal, ICH #9–678–046;

Conpaso Coal Reserve Project, ICH #9-678-152.

3. For an example of such advocacy, see P.O. Gaddis, "The Project Manager," *Harvard Business Review,* May-June 1959, pp. 89-97.

4. For a discussion of the differences between managing MOEs and managing different classes of private firms, see M. Horwitch and C.K. Prahalad, "Managing Technological Innovation—Three Ideal Modes," *Sloan Management Review,* Winter 1976, pp. 77-89.

5. For in-depth and detailed discussions of the American SST program see:

M. Horwitch, "The American SST-A Cautionary Analysis," in *Macro Engineering and the Intrastructure of Tomorrow,* ed. F.P. Davidson et al. (Boulder, CO: Westview Press, 1978);

M. Horwitch, "Managing a Colossus," *The Wharton Magazine,* Summer 1979, pp. 34-41.

M. Horwitch, *Clipped Wings: The American SST Conflict* (Cambridge, MA.: MIT Press, forthcoming).

6. For a more extensive discussion of the American attempt to develop synthetic fuel from coal, see:

M. Horwitch, "Uncontrolled and Unfocused Growth—The U.S. Supersonic Transport Program and the Attempt to Synthesize Fuels from Coal," *Interdisciplinary Science Reviews* (1980):231-244;

M. Horwitch, "Constrained Abundance," in *Energy Future: Report of the Energy Project at the Harvard Business School,* ed. R. Stobaugh and D. Yergin (New York: Random House, 1979), pp. 79-107;

R. Vietor, "The Synthetic Liquid Fuels Program: Energy Politics in the Truman Era," *Business History Review* (Spring 1980);

M. Horwitch and R. Vietor, "The Political Management of Synthetic Fuels: A Retrospective Appraisal" (paper submitted for publication, July 1980).

7. For various early doubts about the current phase for synfuels, see:

E.W. Merrow, S.W. Chapel, and C. Worthing, A Review of Cost Estimation in New Technologies: Implications for Energy Process Plants, ER-2581-DOE (Santa Monica, CA: Rand Corp., July 1979);

Helping Insure Our Future: A Program for Developing Synthetic Fuel Plants Now (New York: Committee for Economic Development, July 29, 1979);

L.J. Carter, "Synfuels Crash Program Viewed as Risky," *Science,* September 7, 1979, pp. 765–766.

8. The data on SITE comes from in-depth field notes by Professor C.K. Prahalad while he was on the Faculty of The Indian Institute of Management in Ahmedabad, India. The research was conducted by Professors A.K. Issac, R.S. Ganapati, and C.K. Prahalad.

9. The UPC is a numerical system with digits for identifying each grocery item by type, manufacturer, and size. The Standard Symbol is a graphical representation to allow for optical-scanning technology for identification and automated check-out purposes. For data on the development of a Universal Product Code and the Standard Symbol in the U.S. grocery industry, see:

Grocery Industry in the U.S.A.: Choice of a Universal Product Code, ICH #9–676–087 Rev. 2/76 (Boston: Intercollegiate Case Clearing House, 1975);

Grocery Industry in the U.S.A.: Choice of a Standard Symbol, ICH #9–677–045 (Boston: Intercollegiate Case Clearing House, 1977).

10. See Horwitch (1980):231–244.

11. See B. McEachron and P.J. Teige, Constraints on Large Scale Technological Projects, Research Report #CSS–4676–14 (Menlo Park, CA: Stanford Research Institute International, 1977).

12. See W.S. Baer, L.L. Johnson, and E.W. Merrow, Analysis of Federally Funded Demonstration Projects: Executive Summary, #R–1925–Doc; Final Report, #R–1926–Doc; and Supporting Case Studies, #R–1927–Doc (Santa Monica, CA: Rand Corp., April 1976):

4

Regulatory and Socioeconomic Factors in the Siting and Construction of Major New Facilities

James S. Hoyte

The discipline of project management has had the benefit of increasingly sophisticated tools and thinking in the years since the basic tools of the critical path method (CPM) and the program evaluation and review technique (PERT) were introduced. Thus, computer-based techniques have become widely and commonly used to help management control projects more effectively. Sophisticated reporting systems are available for monitoring project performance on large-scale and complex projects. Minicomputers permit the project manager in the field to manipulate data quickly and more easily. In addition to the increasing sophistication of computer-based systems, project management has benefited from the application of innovations in organization and behavioral theory.

It may be argued, however, that, despite the availability of these impressive new tools, the project manager is less well equipped today than ever to control cost and schedule. Several commentators on the state of the art of project management have noted that current projects tend to be larger, use more sophisticated technology, and require more complex organizational structures. Even more challenging than the tremendous size and complexity of many current projects is the environment in which such projects often must be managed. Typically, it is the environment more than the project that must be managed. *Environment* is used here in its broadest sense, thereby including the regulatory and sociopolitical atmosphere in which the project occurs. Elements of the project environment that must be taken into account by the project manager if cost and schedule are to be controlled include legal and regulatory requirements, the socioeconomic setting of the project, and citizen participation.

I suggest that the project manager's ability to manage these so-called uncontrollable factors will be the key to project success in the 1980s. In saying *manage,* I choose my words carefully, because I believe that to seek to control rather than manage these factors is not only futile but dangerous. To attempt to control or manipulate today's environmentally aware and sensitive citizenry, for example, is likely to turn a poorly informed project skeptic into an embittered project opponent. Careful attention, however, to the legal and regulatory requirements, potential socioeconomic impacts, the project ecological setting, and the attitudes of the local citizenry during the planning phase will provide the project manager with important data for his management task. Unfortunately, the mere inclusion of these factors in the project plan is not likely to be sufficient. Each factor has elements that are inherently unpredictable and likely to cause schedule slippages, with resulting impact on cost. To minimize the adverse impact of these uncontrollables on project performance, the project-management team should include managers who are skilled in legal analysis and government relations as well as in public affairs and public relations.

At different stages, projects are subject to a variety of laws and regulations at the state, local, and federal level. These laws and regulations may be administered by several different political entities, each with a differing viewpoint of the desirability of the project. To a certain extent, this is true for virtually any construction project, large or small, that might be undertaken in the United States. Thus, the construction of a relatively small industrial plant not only will require compliance with local land-use and zoning laws but is likely to trigger the need for obtaining environmental permits from federal as well as state and local authorities. When a major project is launched, the legal and regulatory requirements are likely to become very significant.

Within the legal and regulatory apparatus that governs projects, environmental concerns have come to play a paramount role. Elaborate mechanisms to review the environmental impact of proposed projects have been established. Since such reviews can have a disastrous impact on the budget and schedule for a project, it is worthwhile to understand in detail the regulatory scheme that has been established for conducting the reviews.

The number of environmental statutes and regulations promulgated in recent years is staggering. At the federal level, the major statutes include the National Environmental Policy Act (NEPA), the Clean Air Act, the Federal Clean Water Act, and the Resource Conservation and Recovery Act (RCRA).[1] There are other federal environmental-review statutes in the United States Code that also can affect the ability to complete a project successfully. Thus, it has been estimated that there are at least thirty federal statutes in addition to NEPA that impose environmental-review requirements.[2]

At the local level, land-use, zoning, and conservation restrictions must be considered in the search for an appropriate site for construction. Furthermore, the local ordinances designed to deal with public health and sanitary issues can be invoked in addition to specific environmental-protection and land-use statutes in an effort to forestall certain kinds of development.

Most states have passed environmental-protection laws and regulations as a supplement to the federal laws of the 1970s. Sometimes, especially in the industrial states, the state environmental-protection regulatory scheme imposes more stringent controls than the federal statutes do. Significant intergovernmental-relations issues can result when differing approaches are pursued by federal and state officials.

This chapter will describe and discuss the regulatory, intergovernmental-coordination, and sociopolitical constraints that can adversely affect the management of medium and large-scale projects. These constraints will be reviewed in the context of the planned construction and operation of a new fossil-fuel-fired power plant. After a description of the federal, state, and local environmental-protection and land-use regulatory framework, the chapter will discuss some of the sociopolitical and intergovernmental-coordination issues that should be of concern to the project manager.

The Federal Regulatory Framework

The National Environmental Policy Act

The National Environmental Policy Act (NEPA) sets a national policy requiring that all federal agencies give comprehensive consideration to environmental impacts in planning and carrying out agency programs. Section 102(2)(C) of the act requires that each federal agency prepare a detailed statement of environmental impact on every major federal action that might significantly affect environmental quality. This environmental impact statement (EIS) must discuss alternatives to the proposed action and must be circulated for comment to other federal agencies, to state and local governments, and to the public.

Title I of the NEPA imposes the environmental review requirement on every federal agency. Title II of the NEPA established the Council on Environmental Quality (CEQ) and with later amendments and supplementary regulations gave it an advisory role over the implementation of the NEPA.

The Environmental Protection Agency (EPA) was created in 1970 pursuant to executive order. The EPA has responsibility for administering the major federal environmental statutes, including those governing air pollution, water pollution, solid and hazardous waste, and noise. Furthermore, the EPA has been given authority to review and comment on all EISs prepared by other federal agencies under the NEPA.

At the core of the NEPA is the requirement that a federal agency prepare and EIS for any major federal action that significantly affects the human environment. The breadth of this jurisdictional concept results in a situation wherein virtually any major construction-project activity is likely to trigger a major federal action, which in turn makes the NEPA applicable to the project unless the activity is categorically excluded. The rationale for the EIS has been set out in the CEQ regulations (40CFR 1502.1) as follows:

> The primary purpose of an environmental impact statement is to serve as an action-forcing device to insure that the policies and goals defined in the Act are infused into the ongoing programs and actions of the Federal Government. It shall provide full and fair discussion of significant environmental impacts and shall inform decision-makers and the public of the reasonable alternatives which would avoid or minimize adverse impacts or enhance the quality of the human environment. Agencies shall focus on significant environmental issues and alternatives and shall reduce paperwork and the accumulation of extraneous background data. Statements shall be concise, clear, and to the point, and shall be supported by evidence that the agency has made the necessary environmental analyses. An environmental impact statement is more than a disclosure document. It shall be used by Federal officials in conjunction with other relevant material to plan action and make decisions."

The EIS process has been widely discussed and criticized, primarily because of the length of time that it can take to complete the process. Federal agencies have attempted to respond to such criticisms by enacting regulations to speed the process. The CEQ, for example, in response to criticism of the length of past EISs, enacted regulations designed to limit the length of EISs (see 40CFR 1502.2).

Although CEQ regulations do not specify if and when public hearings must be held during NEPA review, the NEPA does require that each federal agency consult with and obtain the comments of any other agency (including state and local as well as federal agencies) that has jurisdiction by law or special expertise with respect to any environmental impact involved in the project. Furthermore, public participation in the reveiw process is encouraged, and all outside reviewers are allowed at least forty-five days for their comments.

The actual NEPA-EIS process typically proceeds as follows:

1. A federal agency evaluates a proposed action or program (for example, a grant, subsidy, loan, permit, or license).
2. The agency determines whether its action is categorically excluded.
3. The agency decides that an EIS should be prepared or that an environmental assessment must be prepared to determine whether or not an EIS should be prepared. The environmental assessment may be a major study in itself.
4. After preparation of an environmental assessment, the agency may (1) enter a finding of no significant impact (FNSI) and end the review or (2) decide to prepare an EIS. The agency *must* decide to prepare an EIS for any major federal action significantly affecting the human environment.

If, after completion of an EIS, an agency decides to act by issuing a permit, a funding, or whatever, the agency's decisions in this regard must be accompanied by a record of decision that details the alternatives considered, indicating which were environmentally preferable, and discusses the decision-making process. The record must show whether the environmentally preferable alternative was chosen, and if not, why not. Finally, the document must establish monitoring and mitigation-enforcement mechanisms where appropriate (see 40CFR 1505.2). The regulations require that a decision may not be made less than ninety days after publication of the draft EIS nor less than thirty days after publication of the final EIS.

Note that, while the various activities associated with the NEPA process are being undertaken by federal agencies, the project is suffering from delays and increasing costs. The law is well settled that private parties acting in concert with or by license or permit from federal agencies subject to NEPA may be enjoined from private activities until all EIS requirements are met.[3]

One of the most interesting and important features of the NEPA-EIS process is the opportunity it affords opponents of a project to challenge in court the decisions of federal agencies to allow a project to move forward. Considerable litigation has been spawned by the NEPA, involving challenges by public-interest and environmental groups that object to an agency decision to fund a project or grant a permit. Agencies such as the Department of Housing and Urban Development (HUD), the Army Corps of Engineers, the Nuclear Regulatory Commission (NRC), and many more have been sued under the NEPA. Such suits can bring a project to a standstill.

The Clean Air Act

The Federal Clean Air Act mandates that the EPA regulate the emissions from both stationary and mobile sources of air pollution. In implementing this mandate, the EPA engaged in four major activities:

1. Establishment of concentration limitations for various pollutants in the atmosphere and emission limitations for both stationary- and mobile-source air omissions;
2. Issuance of preconstruction permits covering stationary-source air emissions;
3. Restrictions on the presence or use of certain materials and products that pollute the air; and
4. Review of state plans for attaining EPA's limitations on the concentration of atmospheric pollutants.

The Clean Air Amendments of 1970 required EPA to establish national primary ambient-air-quality standards for various air pollutants. These National Ambient Air Quality Standards (NAAQS) include two concentration levels for each pollutants—a primary standard to protect public health and a secondary standard to protect public welfare. The EPA and the states are to share the responsibility for attaining and maintaining the national standards through a State Implementation Plan (SIP). If a state does not adopt a satisfactory plan, the EPA may act in its stead. An area attaining the NAAQS for a particular pollutant is called an attainment area; an area that exceeds the standard is designated a nonattainment area.

Pursuant to Section 107(C) of the Clean Air Act, the EPA has divided the United States into 247 Air Quality Control Regions (AQCRs), each of which must attain NAAQS. These AQCRs carry the attainment and nonattainment designations for criteria pollutants. The EPA must approve any redesignation of an AQCR for a particular pollutant, a process that is likely to require at least two years of monitoring data showing no violation of the standard. The various states have primary responsibility for meeting the air-quality requirements in the AQCRs within their boundaries. The various policies and regulations that the state uses to carry out this responsibility collectively comprise the SIP.

The Clean Air Act requires the obtaining of various permits, depending on the area affected and the pollutant involved. These permits include the following.

Prevention of Significant Deterioration Permit. In areas where the air quality is cleaner than the NAAQS (attainment areas), the SIP must provide for the prevention of significant deterioration (PSD) of air quality by limiting additional pollution to certain increments above baseline air quality. If a project involves a planned new facility that will affect an attainment area, the project sponsor must obtain a PSD permit before commencing construction. A preconstruction review must be conducted to determine the facility's probable effects on air quality and on growth in the area. In order to secure a permit, the project sponsor must monitor ambient-air-quality data for at least one year, in addition to mathematically modeling the emission impact from the proposed source in order to show no violation of the PSD increments or NAAQS. Emission limitations based on the probable effects of the project and the allowable increment of increased pollution for the particular ACQR will be set in the PSD permit. Furthermore, the pollution source will be required to employ the best available control technology (BACT) for the control of each pollutant, subject to PSD standards. The Clean Air Act provides that an application is to be either approved with conditions or disapproved within one year of submission.

Construction Permit for Nonattainment Area. Under the statute and EPA regulations, no major polluting source may be constructed in a nonattainment area if additional emissions would cause or contribute to a violation of the NAAQS. Before the project sponsor can obtain a construction permit in a nonattainment area he must show the following:

1. The new source will not cause or contribute to violation of emission levels set in the SIP.
2. The new source meets the lowest achievable emission rate (LAER)— that is, the most stringent limitation contained in any SIP for the type of source involved.
3. All major stationary sources owned or operated by the sponsor are in compliance with all applicable air-quality requirements.
4. The SIP is being implemented for the affected nonattainment area.

New Source Performance Standards. Section 111 of the Clean Air Act requires that the EPA publish a list of stationary-source categories that significantly contribute to air pollution and thus could endanger public health or welfare. Furthermore, the EPA is directed to issue emission limitations and standards applicable to new sources within the categories. In response, the EPA has listed and promulgated New Source Performance Standards (NSPS) for plants above a given size in thirty-eight industrial categories, including fossil-fuel-fired steam electric-generating facilities, large boilers and incinerators, pulp mills, and petroleum refineries.[4]

Permit to Construct or Modify Sources of Hazardous Air Pollutants. Section 112(B) of the Clean Air Act requires that the EPA establish limitations on the emissions of hazardous air pollutants from new stationary sources. Hazardous air pollutants are defined as those that may reasonably be expected to result in an increase in mortality or an increase in a serious, irreversible, or incapacitating illness. The EPA has promulgated National Emission Standards for Hazardous Pollutants (NESHAPS)—namely, asbestos, beryllium, mercury, and vinyl chloride. If a project will emit a so-called hazardous air pollutant, a separate permit relating to these pollutants must be obtained.

The Federal Clean Water Act

The principal statute pertaining to water-pollution control is the Federal Clean Water Act (FCWA), which is a substantially amended form of the Federal Water Pollution Control Act of 1972. The FCWA mandates a series of programs designed to address the wide-ranging causes of water pollution. Some of these programs impose detailed regulatory requirements on the discharge of pollutants to waters of the United States; the discharge of dredged or fill material into navigable waters; the discharge of oil and hazardous substances; and the discharge of certain pollutants to treatment works without adequate pretreatment.

The EPA has established effluent limitations for each industry, based on the various levels of technology required by the FCWA. Currently, there are more than 43 categories and 400 subcategories of industries.

Although EPA has primary authority for administering the FCWA, some provisions are administered by the Army Corps of Engineers and the Coast Guard. Furthermore, the FCWA regulatory scheme assumes a strong partnership between the federal government and the state in the implementation of the act.

National Pollutant Discharge Elimination System. The primary means by which the EPA enforces effluent limitations and water quality standards is the National Pollutant Discharge Elimination System (NPDES) permit program. The NPDES program is designed to be delegated by the EPA to the states. This permit sets limitations on effluents that may be discharged and sets dates by which applicable limitations must be met. In accordance with the permit, the project sponsor may be required to install monitoring equipment, maintain records, and exercise the best management practices.

In general, every discharge covered by an NPDES permit will require a level of treatment of its wastes necessary to satisfy the stricter of two standards: (1) technology standards applicable to the facility in question and to the pollutants in the facility's discharge, or (2) standards of water quality prescribed for the segment of water to which the facility is discharging.

Some states, such as Massachusetts, have clean water statutes with regulatory schemes that are closely intertwined with the FCWA implementation program. In Massachusetts, the form used to request an NPDES EPA permit is used by the state regulatory agency, and permits are issued jointly by the EPA and the Massachusetts Division of Water Pollution Control (DWPC).

Water-Quality Certifications. Under Section 401 of the FCWA—as a precondition to the issuance of any license or permit by any federal agency for "any activity, including but not limited to the construction or operation of any facilities," that may result in any discharge into the navigable waters— the state water-pollution-control agency, must certify to the permit-issuing agency that the activity will not have an adverse water-quality impact.

Discharge of Dredge or Fill Material. Pursuant to Section 404 of the FCWA, a permit must be obtained from the U.S. Army Corps of Engineers as a precondition to undertaking any activity involving the discharge of dredge or fill material into navigable waters.

In addition, the Marine Protection, Research and Sanctuaries Act of 1972 (known as the Ocean Dumping Act) requires that a permit be obtained from the EPA for the transportation of materials for dumping in the ocean.

Spills and Discharges of Oil and Hazardous Substances. Numerous federal and state statutes including FWCA, prohibit or provide sanctions for the spilling or discharge of oil or hazardous substances into or near waters.

Resource Conservation and Recovery Act of 1976

The Resource Conservation and Recovery Act of 1976 (RCRA) was enacted to prevent direct environmental damage by regulating the land disposal of both hazardous and nonhazardous wastes. In enacting the RCRA, Congress sought to empower the EPA to regulate those wastes that may harm human health and environment.

Under the RCRA, separate approaches are mandated for the control of hazardous and nonhazardous wastes. The statute charges the EPA with the identification of hazardous wastes; the establishment of a permit program covering the storage, transportation, and disposal of such wastes; and the issuance of guidelines and standards covering the disposal of nonhazardous waste materials.

Section 1004(5) of the RCRA defines hazardous wastes at those solid wastes that cause or significantly contribute to increased mortality or serious, irreversible, or incapacitating illness or that pose a substantial hazard to human health or the environment when improperly treated, stored, transported or disposed of. Solid waste is defined to include all solid, liquid, and contained gaseous waste except domestic sludge, irrigation return flows, permitted point-source discharges under the Federal Water Pollution Control Act, and radioactive materials. All discarded materials that do not fit the definition of hazardous wastes are considered nonhazardous wastes.

The RCRA contemplates a major role for the EPA in the regulation of hazardous wastes, including a full-fledged permit system. The EPA is far behind schedule in implementing comprehensive rules and regulations for the identification of hazardous wastes and standards for generators and transporters of such wastes. If the EPA is, in fact, vigorous in implementing the statutory scheme of the RCRA, project sponsors and managers can expect increased costs and schedule delays for projects that have hazardous-waste by-products. The EPA proposals under consideration would significantly affect the siting and design of power plants and waste-disposal facilities, utility waste-management practices, and capital and operating costs.

Other Federal-Review Requirements

Section 309 of the Clean Air Act empowers the EPA to conduct systematic public review of activities of other agencies, whether or not those projects are covered by an EIS under the NEPA. This provision enables the EPA to review the environmental merits of a proposal, not merely the adequacy of an EIS.

Another very important provision is Office of Management and Budget (OMB) Circular A-95. This procedure is an attempt to provide a comprehensive comment procedure for state and local agencies to meet the requirements of certain provisions of the Demonstration Cities and Metropolitan Development Act of 1966, Title IV of the Inter-governmental Cooperation Act of 1968, and the NEPA.

Under OMB Circular A-95, all applications for federal assistance under more than 150 identified programs must be reviewed and commented on by state and regional clearinghouses *prior to formal application*. Applications by state and local agencies, private and public organizations, and private citizens are all covered by OMB Circular A-95.

The A-95 review considers environmental, social, and economic impacts of proposed projects. Although the state and local agencies cannot veto projects pursuant to this procedure, it does provide such agencies the mechanism to mobilize opposition to federal assistance.

State Regulatory Frameworks

As noted earlier, the statutory scheme for environmental protection and land-use control in the United States tends to result in the involvement of differing agencies at the state, local, and federal levels of government in the review and approval of a project. Each state has developed its own regulatory structure for the review and approval of projects that might have significant environmental impact. Several states, such as Massachusetts, have established state cabinet-level environmental secretariats. Since the Massachusetts approach is by no means unique, the following comments relating to state and local regulation are offered as an example of the type of regulatory approach a project manager might encounter.

The Massachusetts Environmental Protection Act

The Massachusetts Environmental Protection Act (MEPA) was enacted to subject to environmental scrutiny the many governmental activities at the state level (including permit issuance and funding of private action) that have major environmental impact. The statute initially was designed to operate at the state level much as the NEPA operates at the federal level. Both the NEPA and the MEPA provide jurisdiction over certain large projects. Although federal and state agencies usually attempt to coordinate their review activities, there is unfortunately no cross-delegation of responsibilities.[5]

From 1973 through 1977, the MEPA operated similarly to the NEPA, in that agencies prepared the environmental impact review (EIR) and promulgated their own sets of MEPA regulations. Review periods and categorical exclusions were established by each agency, and they varied considerably. Comprehensive amendments enacted in 1977 detailed an MEPA process for uniform applications throughout state agencies.

The MEPA now has a substantive section requiring that each agency, including state boards, departments, commissions, and authorities, and many local authorities, review the impact of their activities on the environment and use all practicable means and measures to minimize or prevent damage to the environment. An agency determination that could be a decision to act or to grant a permit must include a finding describing the impact and a finding that all feasible measures have been taken to avoid or minimize the impact.

Detailed procedures for MEPA review are stated in the remaining statutory sections, which are supplemented by a comprehensive set of MEPA regulations. Briefly, the process involves the following (see figure 4-1):

1. A project is conceived. If the project is private, necessary state actions—permit issuance, approvals, and the like—must be identified. A determination can be made that the MEPA lacks jurisdiction, but, if the determination is in error, a much longer delay may be caused later.

2. Assuming that the project is subject to the MEPA, the requirement for filing is determined by reference to the categorical exclusion regulations that outline the permits, activities, and funding levels requiring MEPA review.

3. A determination must be made of whether or not the project is categorically included with a presumed requirement for an EIR.

4. The MEPA review commences with newspaper publication of a notice of intent and then preparation, circulation, and filing of an Environmental Notification Form (ENF).

5. Publication of the ENF begins a twenty-day period for public and agency comments on whether an EIR should be required for the project and what the EIR should cover. For a private project that is subject to the MEPA only because it requires permits, the scope of the EIR is limited to the subject matter of the permits. Comments are solicited, however, from the public and interested parties.

6. A decision of whether an EIR is required is made by the secretary of

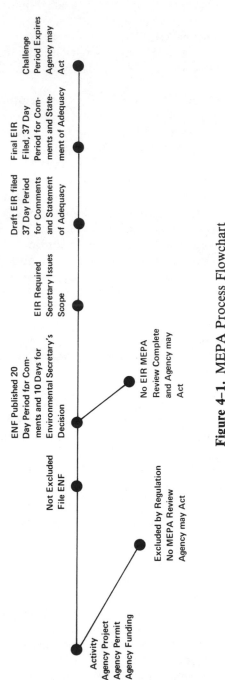

Figure 4-1. MEPA Process Flowchart

environmental affairs within thirty days of publication of the ENF. If an EIR is required, agencies cannot act on the project until after the draft and final EIRs are prepared and reviewed.

7. Under the MEPA, the preparation of the EIR is the responsibility of the project proponent. There are no time limitations on preparation and submission of the EIR.

8. The draft EIR is circulated and filed with the MEPA. Notice is published, commencing a thirty-day comment period. At the close of the comment period, the secretary of environmental affairs must issue within seven days a statement on the adequacy of the draft EIR. Public and agency comments are provided to the proponents. The proponent then prepares a final EIR in response to the secretary's statement and other comments. The final EIR is circulated and filed, and notice is given. After a thirty-day comment period and a seven-day decision period, the secretary may issue a statement of MEPA compliance. The legal challenge period ends sixty days from published notice of the availability of the final EIR, after which agencies may act on the project.

9. Legal challenges under the MEPA may be brought against secretarial decisions that call or do not call for an EIR, delimit a scope, or rule on the adequacy of a draft or final EIR.

Other State Regulatory and Environmental Mechanisms

Massachusetts and most other states have several laws and regulations designed to address specific types of environmental and land-use issues. Specialized environmental statutes typically follow closely similar statutes and regulations at the federal level. These controls at the state level are supplemented by land-use controls at the state and local level that critically affect project-siting decisions.

Rather than attempting to describe or discuss the multitude of specialized environmental and land-use laws and regulations in force in a major state such as Massachusetts, it is sufficient to note that the project manager will be required to interact with numerous state and local governmental entities in order to complete a major project. The variety of requirements is indicated by table 4-1, which provides a partial list of the relevant laws and the implementing agencies in Massachusetts.

Specific Power Plant Siting Laws and Regulations. Other than the selection of nuclear-power-plant sites, the federal government played virtually no role in regulating selection of potential power-plant sites until the 1960s and 1970s. Even now, the federal role in regulating site selection for fossil-fuel power plants is primarily indirect. For nonnuclear facilities, federal concern

Table 4–1
Massachusetts Regulatory Scheme

Statute	Administering Agency
The Massachusetts Clean Air Act	Department of Environmental Quality Engineering
Energy Facilities Siting	Energy Facilities Siting Council
Massachusetts Clean Waters Act	Department of Environmental Quality Engineering
Massachusetts Wetland Protection Act	Department of Environmental Quality Engineering and local conservation commissions
Massachusetts Pesticide Control Act	Mass. Department of Agriculture
Mass. Hazardous Waste Management Act	Department of Environmental Quality Engineering
Mass. Solid Waste Management	Department of Environmental Quality Engineering
Mass. Home Rule and Zoning Act	Local conservation commissions
Subdivision Control Law	Local planning boards
Conservation Restriction Law	Local conservation commissions and Executive Office of Environmental Affairs

has been limited to environmental protection and market regulation. Nevertheless, as the nation's energy problems have become increasingly severe, more direct federal attention has been given to energy-facility siting.

In addition to the EPA's regulatory role under the NEPA, the two federal agencies that play significant roles in power-plant-facility site selection are the Nuclear Regulatory Commission (NRC) and the Department of Energy (DOE), through the Federal Energy Regulatory Commission (FERC).

The FERC, which superseded and took over the powers of the Federal Power Commission in 1977, has principal responsibility for regulating public utilities that produce and sell electricity on the interstate market. Although most of the FERC's activities relate to rate regulation rather than to facility site selection, FERC policies do significantly affect the construction of new power plants. FERC policies regarding allowance of construction work in progress in the site base, encouragement of superregional power-supply systems, and fuel conversion will influence construction.

The environmental movement of the 1960s and 1970s resulted in the extensive involvement of many state, local, and federal regulatory agencies in the project-siting decision. This involvement was particularly great with respect to siting of industrial plants and electric-power plants. The review activities of numerous agencies, each with its own specific area of concern, resulted in increasing complexity and long construction lead times (see table 4–2). In fact, each local, state, or federal independent regulatory agency involved with the siting, construction, or initial operation of a facility possessed the power, through expressed environmental concern, to halt a project.

The alarm caused by this trend toward project cessation, especially in light of a newly understood severe energy crisis, led to a movement at the state level toward enactment of specialized energy-facility-siting legislation. In general, the goal of such legislation has been to streamline the site-selection process through consolidation and coordination of all governmental review and regulatory activities within one state power-siting commission. In reality, the energy-facilities-siting councils and commissions have achieved uneven results in facilitating project initiation, project execution, and project completion.

It is difficult to pinpoint the reasons why so-called one-step siting at the state level has not had the desired results. Certainly, part of the problem has been ongoing bureaucratic infighting by established environmental and local land-use-control agencies that have resisted politically the usurpation

Table 4–2
Selected Federal Agencies Involved in Project Regulation and Review

U.S. Army Corps of Engineers

Council on Environmental Quality

Department of Agriculture
    Forest Service

Departments of Commerce
    National Oceanographic and Atmospheric Agency
    Coastal Zone Management Program

Department of Defense

Department of the Interior
    Bureau of Indian Affairs
    Fish and Wildlife Service
    Bureau of Land Management
    National Park Service

Department of Housing and Urban Development

Department of Transportation

Department of Energy
    Federal Energy Regulatory Commission

Environmental Protection Agency

Federal Aviation Administration

Nuclear Regulatory Commission

Securities and Exchange Commission

of their power by these energy-facility-siting bodies. In addition, although the public increasingly recognizes the energy-scarcity problem, consumers continue to be extremely critical of what some view as poor managerial planning and improper resource utilization by the utilities. This sentiment has led to even more vigorous attempts by various groups to use the regulatory process to stop construction of new utilities. The multitude of environmental and land-use laws and regulations continues to provide the mechanism for expressing such opposition.

Other Constraining Externalities. The environmental and land-use-control laws and regulations have provided mechanisms for interested parties to focus on issues that are external to projects but nevertheless capable of strongly affecting them. Citizen participation in project-siting decisions has been evident to some degree, especially at the local level, through planning-board and zoning hearings. Not until the explosion in environmental controls of the 1960s and 1970s, however, did the impact of such participation really begin to be felt.

The very multiplicity of regulatory agencies has caused significant problems of intergovernmental relations, which have an adverse impact on projects. Regulatory agencies that have accumulated responsibilities without corresponding increases in resources have been slow in reaching decisions that are crucial to the status of a project's schedule and budget. Similarly, some agencies that have been established hurriedly to implement new environmental controls have had inadequate time to absorb and understand the implications of their new responsibilities. Some agencies have been given somewhat conflicting missions—as both promoter of an industry and regulator of the industry's behavior.

The geographical setting for a proposed project can be constraining in several ways. Projects undertaken in heavily populated areas pose the problem of execution with minimum disruption of people's daily lives. The construction process itself is an irritant that invites citizen opposition. Such settings have the advantage, however, of an existing infrastructure to provide resources and services to the project team.

When a project must be undertaken in a remote and hostile environment, such as arctic or desert areas, the infrastructure problems may become unmanageable. Conceivably, the geographic setting may be unique to the project participants and so remote that there is no way to anticipate the particular laboring challenge posed by that setting. Thus, the constructors of the Trans Alaskan pipeline system had to build in areas where no one had previously worked and under conditions that were impossible to simulate.

Largely because of the environmental concerns discussed earlier, the sponsors of large-scale energy projects have located such projects as far as possible from major population centers. Location of such projects in remote areas may minimize the likelihood that adverse public opinion will be mobilized against the project. The massive yet temporary nature of such projects, however, is likely to accentuate the project's impact on the remote community. Although the residents of such communities are generally likely to be project boosters—welcoming the economic stimulation that the project is likely to cause—a legitimate question may be raised regarding whether the long-run impact will be salutory. In fact, courts have held that project planners must consider and attempt to minimize problems that might be caused by the temporary influx of many construction workers and their dependents into a rural area whose local government and other resources may be unable to provide essential goods and services. An interesting, if somewhat glamorous, example of such a project situation occurred when the 1980 Winter Olympics came to Lake Placid, New York. Licensing authorities dealing with much more mundane projects have been held to have a duty to take socioeconomic factors into consideration during the environmental-impact assessment process.[6]

The NEPA has provided the principal vehicle for active public participation in project-related decision making. Although there is only very brief mention of public participation in the NEPA, the agency-review requirements of the NEPA have resulted in intensive and extensive citizen involvement in the federal, state, and local decision-making process. The encouragement of public participation in the EIS process has become a basic tenet of most state and federal agencies. The legal requirements in the NEPA are not only that the EIS be reviewed by appropriate federal, state, and local agencies but also that copies of the EIS be made available for public review. In addition, federal, state, and local agencies with permit-issuance or other regulatory responsibility generally have a legal requirement to hold a public hearing before taking action.

Most major projects, especially new power-plant-construction projects, generate strong public interest and opposition. The opponents are likely to include local citizens directly affected by project location, conservationists and wildlife enthusiasts, vested-interest groups, consumers or rate payers, and activists who generally oppose any major new construction. Federal environmental laws and regulations have institutionalized citizen participation in the project-development process. Furthermore, the decade of the 1970s saw the growth of numerous public-interest groups with the avowed purpose of monitoring or stopping large-scale development projects. Although many such groups are extremely well informed and usually very well organized, others are inaccurately informed and undisciplined.

It is essential that the project-management team possess the capability to determine the character of the citizen groups with which it must deal and manage its relationship with the group accordingly. The project manager should know whether interactions with citizen groups are to be primarily for educational, negotiation, or planning purposes.

Conclusion: The Impact of Regulatory Process on Projects

To assess the impact of the various laws and regulations on project performance, the regulatory requirements that must be met in constructing and operating a new coal-fired electric-generating plant were described. Other possible examples might include a nuclear-power plant, a solid-waste-treatment facility, or a petrochemical plant. A coal-fired electric-generating plant was chosen partly because such projects should benefit from the national commitment to the increased use of coal for electric generation as part of the overall strategy of lessening U.S. dependence on imported oil.

Regardless of regulatory complications, the process of planning and constructing a new coal-fired power plant is lengthy and expensive. Assuming completion of a preplanning feasibility study that might take six or more months and cost more than $100,000, one can expect a site-selection program of approximately eighteen months, costing $150,000 to $500,000. The next activities—which might include detailed environmental evaluation of three alternate sites, obtaining sites, obtaining site access and options, and conceptual engineering—could extend over two years at a cost of more than $3 million, exclusive of options on land. Allowing one year for regulatory-agency review of plans and issuance of preconstruction permits when no opposition exists, the project will have been subject to five years of preconstruction time at a cost of $4 million. Actual land acquisition, final engineering, and equipment-and-supply procurement can then proceed. Construction of the first unit might begin eighteen to twenty-four months after power-plant permits are issued and might be completed in six years. Thus, the time span from initial concept to completion of construction can run ten to twelve years under the best regulatory circumstances, assuming that no environmental problems or objections are raised.

Notes

1. The National Environmental Policy Act, 42 U.S.C. §§ 4321 et seq.; The Clean Air Act, 42 U.S.C. §§ 1857 et seq.; the Clean Water Act, 33 U.S.C. §§ 1251 et seq.; the Resource Conservation and Recovery Act, 42 U.S.C. 6900 et seq.

2. See Rosenberg and Olson, Federal Environmental Review: Requirements Other Than NEPA, the Emerging Challenge, 27 *Cleveland State Law Review* 195 (1978).

3. See Silva v. Romney, 473 F.2d 287 (1st Cir. 1973); Boston Water-front Residents Association v. Romney, 343 F. Supp. 89 (D. Mass. 1972).

4. See, generally, Truitt and Abeles, Coal-Fired Electric Generating Facilities: Impediments Under Federal Environmental Legislation, 11 *St. Mary's Law Journal* 609 (1980), and Cooke, "Air and Noise Pollution and Radiation," in *Environmental Law and Land Use Control,* MCLE-NELI (1980).

5. This section draws heavily from the work of Mygatt, "Environmental Impact Review: NEPA and MEPA," in *Environmental Law and Land Use Control,* MCLE-NELI (1980).

6. See, generally, Watson, Measuring and Mitigating Socio-Economic Environmental Impacts of Constructing Energy Projects: An Emerging Regulatory Issue, 10 *Natural Resources Lawyer* 393.

5 Research and Development: A Changing Federal Perspective

James Costantino

The changing character of the economic and energy environment is enlarging the scope of federal research needs beyond the traditional agenda of technology problems and is posing new challenges to the R&D project manager. Research and development management will not be on a business-as-usual basis in the future.

Anyone who tries to discuss in some depth the future of R&D faces large problems, including what Scammon and Wattenberg call the "Law of Simultaneous but Contrary Truths"[1]—simply stated, that, although this is true, so is that, but that somehow the two truths do not always coincide, especially in the federal establishment. Concepts of the future in the bureaucracy seldom extend with any confidence or authority beyond the next appropriations cycle.

One important thing we have learned is that the real solutions to our country's problems are not solely technological, they also involve economic and institutional considerations. In the 1960s and 1970s, the U.S. government seemed to have an unending supply of money and the organizations to spend it. Furthermore, taxpayers did not mind spending it on high-technology programs, such as space research, nuclear aircraft, and magnetically levitated trains.

Alvin Toffler, author of *Future Shock*[2] and *The Third Wave*,[3] reminds us that technological decisions are inherently political. More and more people are demanding the right to participate in the decision-making process, and they have demonstrated this right in tangible ways that we all understand: California's Proposition 13; Massachusetts' Proposition 2½; and, in a major way in the last election, the voters' support for President Reagan's supply-side economic policies. Thus, R&D managers can no longer think about customers as merely the users of whatever is being sold. They are also citizens, workers, dreamers, human beings; above all, they are taxpayers.

One of the most critical problems facing private-sector R&D managers, especially those who receive federal funding directly or indirectly, is understanding the complex interrelationships between technical managers and the federal government in R&D. Governmental R&D policies in the 1980s will

57

make a great deal of difference in how managers, their firms, and the private sector bring about product and process innovation—that is, develop new products, invest in needed equipment and facilities, and get the products into the marketplace.

The issue of industrial decline and its challenge to U.S. industrial policy, which will be one of the major concerns of the 1980s, is most visible in the automotive sector. In 1980, domestic automobile producers posted aggregate losses of more than $4 billion. Meanwhile, Japan, for the first time in history, sold more automobiles to the world than the United States did. Plagued by the reality, or at least the image, of high prices and poor quality, the U.S. automobile industry now faces the grim task of having to invest $80 billion by 1985 just to keep even with the Japanese, who already have a landed cost advantage of $1,000 to $1,500 per vehicle.

While the economists debate whether the problem is cyclical or structural, and the business schools write cases on an industry that seemingly could not foresee the foreseeable, almost a million jobs in the automotive sector have disappeared. Some people seem content to write off the automobile industry as a bad debt, suggesting that we focus our energies on the so-called sunrise industries. Unfortunately, however, the problems faced by the automotive sector are symptomatic of the problems faced by many of our basic industries, such as steel, aluminum, rubber, and components, as well as our technological leaders, such as computers, semiconductors, and aircraft. All these industries are or will be facing the determined foreign onslaught as Japan implements its vision of the 1980s, which will further restructure the Japanese economy to emphasize knowledge-intensive products. European governments will also be hard at work stimulating industrial successes in consumer electronics, automated manufacturing equipment, biotechnologies, and various innovations to achieve energy conservation.

Because our foreign competitors understand that technological innovation is a primary source of economic growth, they have adopted policies that promote this process. Moreover, the R&D activities of foreign governments are targeted toward enhancing their own industrial efficiency and competitiveness. Priority goals include the development of knowledge-intensive production systems, optical communication, very large scale integrated circuits, laser technology, new materials, and aerospace technology. Thus, R&D management in this country in the 1980s must be considered within the broader context of an environment that is not only domestic but also international.

The United States' loss of technological leadership, however, cannot be blamed on insufficient R&D funding. Actual R&D expenditures in the United States far exceed those of all other countries, with the exception of the USSR. In fact the United States spends more on R&D than do the United Kingdom, France, West Germany, and Japan combined.

How, then, can we reconcile this nation's dismal economic performance with its comparatively massive investment in R&D? The answer seems to lie in at least two major flaws associated with the way we have been doing our R&D business in this country.

First, our R&D efforts seem to be uncoupled from global markets. In the United States, about half of all R&D funding is provided by government, and two-thirds of these expenditures are defense- and space-oriented. In West Germany and Japan, in contrast, industry provides a majority of R&D funding, and any government R&D funding is highly concentrated in areas directly related to economic growth—manufacturing processes, telecommunications, and transportation technologies. It has become apparent that technological advantage is not solely based on invention but also is linked to the pace with which new technologies can be adapted for consumer markets. It seems that an emphasis on technology creation, as opposed to commercialization, leads to a nation of inventors, not a nation of innovators. That may be why Great Britain has captured so many Nobel prizes and yet is plagued with poor productivity. Japan, however, has won few Nobel prizes but is highly productive and internationally competitive. Japan is excellent at adaptive R&D, as opposed to basic research, of which it does very little.

Second, now that the World War II and Korean War babies have entered the work force, we find that we may have become a nation of technical illiterates. At a time when the role of technology is at a high level throughout our society, many high school and college graduates are without science and mathematics training beyond the tenth grade. The deemphasis on science and mathematics in our schools in the postwar years is in sharp contrast to education in other industrialized countries. The strength of Japanese engineering is rooted in Japan's high level of technical education. Japan has emphasized and will continue to emphasize the skills required by a technology-based economy.

Furthermore, any engineering school dean will agree that we are damaging our future when we make it more financially rewarding for new engineering graduates to move directly into industry rather than to stay in school and work on their master's degrees and doctorates. The number of engineering doctorates awarded by U.S. universities declined 20 percent between 1974 and 1978. Aggravating this trend is the growth in the number and proportion of degrees awarded to foreign students, many of whom will return home when their educations are completed. In effect, the United States is exporting an increasing proportion of its vital technological infrastructure—at a time when the national need is so great.

Not only do we need to train a new generation of American technologists in such areas as automation, robotics, computer-aided design, production processes, and quality assurance, but our universities also need up-to-date equipment and staffs. Before World War II, almost 90 percent of the research effòrt in universities was supported by industry and 5 percent by the government. Those numbers are now reversed; over 90 percent of university research support comes from government and only 5 percent from industry. As a result, university research has become progressively divorced from industrial concerns. To compete in global markets, it will be necessary to bring about closer interaction between universities and industry. Only then can we couple the ingenuity residents in academia to our emerging global technical challenges in the 1980s.

In the past, uncertainties associated with health impacts, safety, and various mandated performance requirements have cast a cloud over the introduction of new technologies. They have retarded the diffusion rates, increased the start-up costs, and confined the potential markets. The attendant increase in risk and cost has had a tremendous impact on R&D, causing it to become defensive and incremental rather than hard-hitting and far-reaching. In an era of global competition, we can no longer afford the luxury of surrendering technological leadership by default.

It is clear that the United States is in a period of technological reassessment. New goals and concerns have replaced those of the 1960s and 1970s. We can no longer continue making decisions that are self-defeating and injurious to our industrial base.

What does all this mean for federal R&D? I believe that, with the notable exception of defense and perhaps space research, the government will substantially decrease its hardware development, leaving that to the private sector. Thus, federal R&D funding will be used for knowledge generation, not for hardware generation. The government will be conducting and funding anticipatory and informational research to guide federal policy and decision making in areas wherein it is appropriate for the federal government to be making policy and decisions. Otherwise, federal decisions cannot be responsive to the rapidly changing world industrial situation. Business as usual cannot mean lurching from crisis to crisis in an interdependent and international marketplace.

Beneath the flesh of all the rhetoric, however, there usually is a skeleton of principle. We have now stepped back to take a look at ourselves, and we are not totally satisfied with what we see. As taxpayers, however, we must not be too anxious to change the entire system overnight, or we risk losing important positive factors with the negative.

Notes

1. Richard M. Scammon and Ben J. Wattenberg, *The Real Majority* (New York: Coward, McCann and Geoghegan, 1971).
2. Alvin Toffler, *Future Shock* (New York: Random House, 1970).
3. Alvin Toffler, *The Third Wave* (New York: Morrow, 1980).

6

Management, Innovation, and Technology

Robert C. Seamans, Jr.

Constraints on managers and executives often inhibit innovation and the use of developing technology. As a result, there has been marked deterioration of competitive vigor in many American businesses relative to foreign competition. Hayes and Abernathy note that economists and business leaders attribute our economic ills to "the rapacity of OPEC, deficiencies in government tax and monetary policies, and proliferation of regulation."[1] How does this explain, however, a decline in our rate of growth compared to that of Europe and Japan? Experience suggests that success now requires an organizational commitment to compete over the long run by offering superior products and services. Hayes and Abernathy conclude, however, that our present managerial gospel encourages short-term cost reduction rather than long-term development of technological competitiveness.

Uses of New Technology

It is difficult enough to maintain a position in existing businesses by innovation in processing and products, but even more difficult in determining what new products and businesses should be developed. Clearly, this is more difficult partly because of the problems of entry into untested markets. In the 1930s, Vannevar Bush designed and tested a differential analyzer at the Massachusetts Institute of Technology (MIT) and, in the early 1940s, three large, general-purpose digital computers were built for ballistic computations and other calculations needed to support developments in World War II. It is fortunate that IBM, Control Data Corporation and other manufacturers did not rely on the market survey taken at that time. A committee reviewing the need for computer capability comparable to that provided by these machines estimated that the United States might require as many as ten such machines in the future, primarily for military and scientific devices, and so forth, have created unimagined markets, and we are now in a major technological race with Europe and Japan to maintain our share of this expanding market.

Thus, MIT is considering a new laboratory for research on the application of very large scale integrated circuits, a technology that is intimately related to computer capability. The design of chips with 70,000 or more elements relies heavily on computers, and future computers will contain myriad of chips.

Other rapidly developing technologies include the following:

Computer-aided design and manufacture (CAD/CAM). Industry already has a major effort under way in this area. Even though the U.S. automotive industry may not be producing competitive small cars, its use of computer graphics is impressive. Designs are now filed not as drawings but as codes in a computer.

Complex controls. Control systems for the aircraft of the 1940s operated with single feedback loops. Now, with new electronic technology, these systems use quadruple redundant feedback for the actuators that affect the safety of aircraft. In spacecraft of the future, hundreds of feedback elements will be used to stabilize large, flexible structures.

Gas turbines. The internal-combustion engine for aircraft has given way to the gas turbine, but will the automobile follow suit? The turbine offers greater fuel flexibility and also has higher efficiency if operating temperatures can be increased. The question remains whether ceramic components can be manufactured at sufficiently low cost for automotive use.

Composite structures. Metals in transportation systems are being replaced by composites that are strengthened with carbon and boron fibers.

Biotechnology. It is impossible to predict what biotechnology may have in store. Synthetic insulin is now being tested on human subjects at Eli Lilly. In the future, genetic techniques may be applied not only to pharmaceuticals but to chemicals, energy extraction and processing, waste treatment, and agriculture.

I do not propose to give a complete listing of all possible technological developments, but the many changes needed in the field of energy supply and demand provide a good illustration.

Prior to the 1973–1974 energy embargo, the use of energy was increasing at a rate of 3.5 percent per year, and our economy, as measured by the gross national product (GNP), was expanding at 4.7 percent per year. As a result of the embargo, both energy use and the GNP declined several percentage points, and unemployment increased by nearly one million.[2] Following the embargo, energy consumption increased 5 percent, and the economy expanded at 6 percent until 1978. Since then, the economy has flagged as the energy-growth rate has dropped to 1 percent, and we are importing oil at the astronomical annual level of $80 billion to $90 billion. This imbalance in payments cannot continue without jeopardizing our economy and national security. Even with strenuous resolve to use energy more efficiently and to increase domestic supplies by major increases in coal and nuclear production, there will be a continued shortfall of energy for transportation needs unless there is a major conversion to synthetic fuels.[3]

During World War II, Germany relied heavily on synthetic oil and gas derived from coal, but the technology has not been greatly improved since then because of the cheap, plentiful supply of natural gas and oil. There are many potential barriers to a large-scale synthetic-fuel industry, including uncertainty in the technology, limitations in coal transportation, risks to the environment, amounts of capital required, and high operating costs. In my view, the government must assist in starting this new industry, but progress ultimately will depend on industrial initiative.[4] In January 1975, President Ford recommended to the Congress that the government support a million-barrel-per-day synthetic-fuel industry. Detailed review led to a request for $6 billion in loan guarantees to initiate a variety of plants, with a total capacity of 300,000 barrels per day. Although the request passed overwhelmingly by the Senate, it was soundly defeated by the House in 1975 and again, narrowly, in 1976. In 1980, the Congress supported the Carter administration's proposal for the Synthetic Fuels Corporation and for a Department of Energy cost-sharing program for two 20,000-barrel-per-day solvent-refined coal plants. This so-called SRC program, costing an estimated $2 billion, has subsequently been rescinded by the Reagan administration. If not restored by the Congress, I predict that it will be reinitiated by this administration after a hiatus of a year or two.

Impact on the Engineering Profession

In this period of low growth in our economy, the energy situation is expected to lead to major growth in the engineering profession, even without a new synthetic-fuel industry. During the past eight years, the undergraduate enrollment in engineering schools has risen from 185,000 to over 300,000, and there now is a demand for even more. At MIT, we continually ask ourselves what the future role of engineers will be.[5] Clearly, the engineering need will be different in the 1980s and 1990s than it has been in the past. I find it helpful to divide the engineering profession into five categories: (1) engineering scientist, (2) practicing engineer, (3) entrepreneurial engineer, (4) management engineer, and (5) systems engineer. These categories are not completely separate and distinct, however, and their roles are changing with time. The systems engineer, for example, originally dealt with complex problems, such as the design of a missile, that involved more than one type of engineering, such as electronics, hydraulics, propulsion, and aerodynamics. Currently, the role of the systems engineer must be even broader, and he or she often must have an understanding of toxicology, economics, sociology, and even politics.

The basic concept of a recent Harvard University project known as MATEP (Medical Area Total Energy Plant) was sound technically, if not institutionally. The plant will deliver chilled water, steam, and electricity to the Harvard Medical School, the Harvard School of Public Health, and seven neighboring hospitals. In this way, the heat normally wasted in electric-power generation will be used by the participating institutions. Unfortunately, the construction of the plant was delayed for several years because of concerns in the adjacent residential area about the increased nitrogen oxides that might be emitted into the neighboring atmosphere. In addition and for a variety of reasons—including the need for more complete emission controls—the cost of the project increased by almost ten times, to its present total of nearly a quarter of a billion dollars. The director of the program recently gave his version of the six phases of such a large systems project: (1) enthusiasm, (2) disillusionment, (3) panic, (4) search for the guilty, (5) punishment for the innocent, and (6) delayed, high-cost completion.

Perhaps Harvard should not try to provide its own utilities, but the story is not very different at the Seabrook nuclear facility and many other locations. Nuclear power is considered the enemy, and fossil fuel, particularly coal, is also in disrepute.

Role of the U.S. Government

A decline in U.S. productivity clearly has become a government concern. Bills have been proposed in the Congress to establish a National Technology Foundation, to be set up in parallel with the National Science Foundation. The question asked is: If NASA can take us to the moon, why cannot government take the lead in improving the innovative process? The answer is basic. It is up to industry, not government, to take the initiative; industry must manage the use of technology more creatively. Government also has a number of key responsibilities, however.[6] It must institute policies and regulations that provide incentives for the investor or that at least remove unnecessary disincentives. In addition, government, along with industry, should provide support for research and education and should help underwrite high-risk ventures of national importance, such as synthetic fuels. Finally, government must finance long-term activities, such as the fusion program.

Industry can learn lessons from the Apollo program.[7] First, industry must lay the groundwork for future innovation, as was done in NASA's hydrogen-research program in the 1950s. Research on coal is today's equivalent. Industry also must be willing to take calculated risks, as was done, for example, in the prelaunch digital checkout for Apollo. (General Sarnoff also took a calculated risk when he invested $500 million and the future of RCA to provide compatible color television. High-risk developments in industry must have a backup, as was provided, for example, for the Nova booster for direct ascent versus orbital rendezvous and docking approaches. Finally, managers must be willing to accept new approaches, even in the middle of the project, John Houbolt and a small group of zealots at the Langley Research Center never gave up on lunar-orbit rendezvous. This view is controversial, however, some favor freezing the design early and only using state-of-the-art technology. Clearly, changes in a large program must be made in a disciplined fashion.

Change and the use of new technologies can cause delays and may cost more at the time, thus reducing short-term profits, but it is often the only way to succeed. In referring to the space program, President Kennedy cited a story by Frank O'Connor, an Irish writer, about his youth:

> As a boy, O'Connor and his friends would make their way across the countryside, and when they came to an orchard wall that seemed too high and too doubtful to try and too difficult to permit their voyage to continue, they took off their hats and tossed them over the wall—and then they had no choice but to follow.
>
> This Nation has tossed its cap over the wall of space, and we have no choice but to follow it. . . . With the help and support of all Americans, we will climb the wall with safety and speed, and we shall then explore the wonders on the other side.[8]

If management is not prepared to toss its hat over the wall—to innovate and to take the risks—it must be prepared to lose business in domestic and foreign markets. Our ability to compete in the future depends on the rapid development and use of new technology and new approaches.

Notes

1. Robert T. Hayes and William F. Abernathy, "Managing Our Way to Economic Decline," *Harvard Business Review* 58, no. 4 (July–August 1980).

2. Energy Reorganization Act of 1974, Public Law 93–483, 93rd Congress, 11 October 1974, Section 2(a); Federal Nonnuclear Energy Research and Development Act of 1974, Public Law 93–577, 93rd Congress, 31 December 1974, Section 2(c).

3. "A National Plan for Energy Research, Development and Demonstration: Creating Energy Choices for the Future." Volume I: "The Plan;" Volume II: "Program Implementation, Energy Research and Development Administration," Report ERDA-48 (Washington, D.C., 1975), and Report ERDA-76-1 (Washington, D.C., 1976).

4. R.C. Seamans, Jr., and F.I. Ordway, "Energy's Challenge to Aerospace," *Journal of Energy* 2 (March–April, 1978).

5. R.C. Seamans, Jr., and K.F. Hansen, "Engineering Education for the Future," *Technology Review* 83 (February–March, 1981).

6. "Pacing Systems of the Apollo Program," Subcommittee on NASA Oversight of the Committee on Science and Astronautics, U.S. House of Representatives, 89th Congress, First Session, Serial K, (Washington, D.C.: U.S. Government Printing Office, 1965); H. B. Finger and A.F. Siepert, "NASA Management of the Civilian Space Program," Paper presented at the Sixteenth International Conference of the Institute for Management Sciences, New York, 26–28 March 1969; "Apollo Program Management," Subcommittee on NASA Oversight of the Committee on Science and Astronautics, U.S. House of Representatives, 91st Congress, First Session, Serial C (Washington, D.C.: U.S. Government Printing Office, 1969); R.C. Seamans, Jr., "Action and Reaction," The 1969 Minta Martin Lecture, Massachusetts Institute of Technology, Cambridge, 1969).

7. R.C. Seamans, Jr., and F.I. Ordway, "The Apollo Tradition: An Object Lesson for the Management of Large-scale Technological Endeavors," *Interdisciplinary Science Reviews* 2 (No. 4), 1977.

8. Remarks by John F. Kennedy at the Rededication of the Aerospace Medical Health Center, San Antonio, Texas, November 21, 1963.

Part III
Strategy and Planning

7

Strategic Factors in Project-Based Businesses

John R. White

Program-management methods have been developed to meet the needs of undertakings characterized by a specified duration and content; there is a fundamental difference in the activities required to construct a building, for example, and those required to produce refrigerators. Within the category of programs, however, there seem to be several subsets with different characteristics that are important to the strategies of competitors in the field. Figure 7-1 shows a sorting of programs according to the numbers of products and projects they contain. The four categories are as follows:

1. The first classification is unique projects, such as laying the Atlantic cable, or laying the Alyeska pipeline. Although they should not, certain nuclear-power-plant projects develop a one-project, one-product character. acter.

2. The second category involves replication of similar projects. The design and construction of process plants, buildings, dams, and fossil-fuel power plants, for example, involve many projects providing essentially the same product. Typical in this category would be a company that specializes in process plants building similar petrochemical plants over the years under a series of different projects for different customers.

3. The third type is a single project with a variety of products. An example is the Apollo program, which was one long program with manned space shots for various purposes.

4. Finally, there are multiple projects involving different though similar products. The production of a particular aircraft model would be an example of one such project and product. A company providing the product over time would design new aircraft that, though similar, would be like different products in many ways.

These four kinds of programs appear to have different strategic characteristics; that is, some of their characteristics suggest that they move by different competitive rules. A consideration of learning curves gives us the situations shown in figure 7-2. The one-project–one-product undertaking of case 1 in the figure by definition, has no overall learning curve. We cannot say, for example, that the fourth pipeline takes 72 percent of the man-hours that were required to build the first because there is only one. Fortunately, there are repeated steps within the project whereby learning bene-

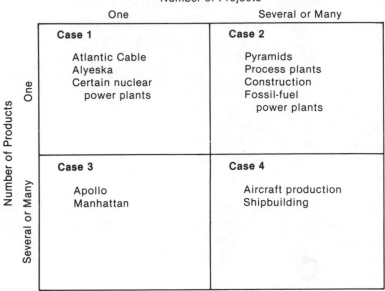

Figure 7–1. Characteristic Types of Programs

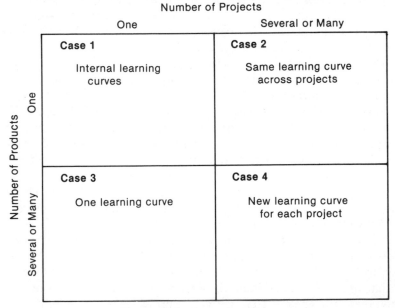

Figure 7–2. Learning Curves

fits can be achieved. The design, fabrication, and erection of vertical-support members is an example from the Alyeska project. Pipe welding in nuclear-power-plant construction is another. The competitive related factor is the contractor's skill in managing the application of learning to the sequence of seemingly different component parts of the project.

In case 2 wherein many projects are replicating essentially the same product, we expect to find the same learning curve operating across projects for certain cost elements. A key competitive factor would be how many projects had been completed previously.

In the single-project–several-product programs of case 3, we would look for one learning curve threading its way through the multiple replicated products—as, in the Apollo project, the various shots from suborbital to moon landing.

In case 4, we find a new learning curve for each project. Even though a new aircraft is similar to its predecessor, and the labor cost in man-hours per pound for the first plane and the hundredth plane will track a similar curve, each starts over at the beginning.

To the extent that learning curves, cost, and market share are related in a positive-feedback loop, as they are in some industries, share would have the significance shown in figure 7-3. Clearly, in a single-project world (cases 1 and 3), share has no meaning and does not exist as such, certainly at the prime contractor level. For multiple projects involving a single product or very similar products (case 2), share plays its conventional, well-known role in competitive strength. Where there are essentially different products for each project, the learning curve itself, rather than position on it in the usual sense, is competitive significant; that is, in case 4, a firm's project learning curve is one of the bases of competition.

These observations seem to be intimately related to industry characteristics. In the more usual sense, there does not seem to be a single-project industry. There may be a pipeline-construction industry, and it probably belongs in case 2 of figure 7-4, but the Alyeska pipeline does not belong in that category. Similar remarks could be made about the Apollo program and the aerospace industry.

We can however, identify industries for the multiple-project activities. Those in case 2 appear to belong to conventionally defined industries. Since share changes its strategic role depending on whether the industry is concentrated or fragmented, it is useful to inquire into that question for activities in case 2. Examination of industry data for general, heavy-industrial or process-plant construction suggests that the industry is on the borderline between fragmented and concentrated, so this will be an important matter to clarify with respect to a specific industry.

Activities in case 4 belong to what have been called geyser industries— a company moves along with its resources, looking for contracts, and every

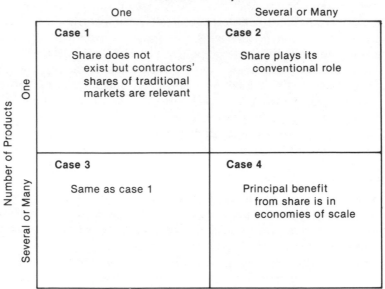

Figure 7–3. Role of Market Share

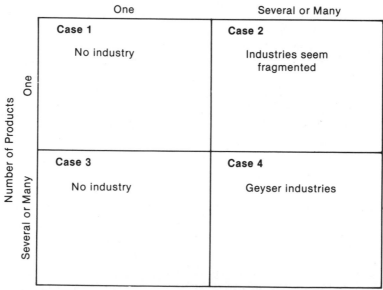

Figure 7–4. Industry Types

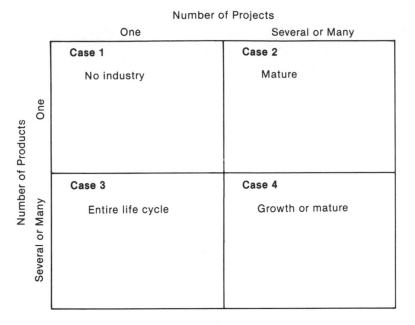

Figure 7–5. Industry Maturity

once in awhile wins a winner-take-all program and is set for a few years. Share does not seem to play a dominant role in determining relative competitive position, although, of course, the stronger competitors tend to hold the larger share of the available market. Share is the effect, however, not the cause. It would appear that these industries do not have a positive-feedback loop at work. In fact, high share can block new awards as the government seeks to maintain the defense-industry base and to spread business among constituencies.

An exploration of industry leads us naturally to the question of industry maturity, as sketched in figure 7–5. Again, in case 1 there is no industry. The industries in case 2 seem very mature, which is compatible with the characteristic role of share in these industries.

We said earlier that the activities in case 3 had no industry. Our example of Apollo brings to mind the words *embryonic* and *growth,* but I think these are suggested by the technology rather than by characteristics of the industry. Embryonic technologies can exist in industries of any maturity, of course, and the same can be said for mature technologies. All that can be said about the single-program activity is that it goes through an entire life

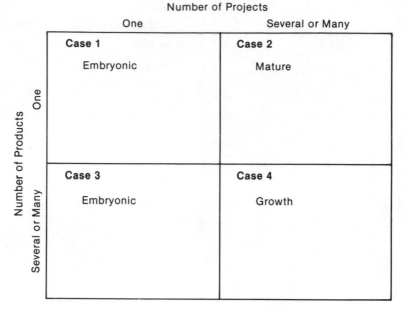

Figure 7–6. State of Technology

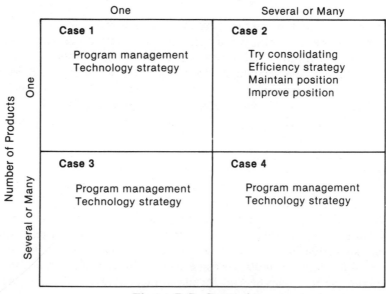

Figure 7–7. Strategies

cycle over the course of the project. Thus, Apollo started out as an infant in 1961 and ended up dead in 1972.

I would argue that the geyser industries are in either a growth or mature stage, because achieving program stage is one sign of arriving at the growth phase. Conversely, by the time an industry is aging, it is likely that the product will be purchased—army blankets, for example, rather than airplanes.

Figure 7-6 suggests a broad generalization about the state of technology in each of the types of programs. This is a generality because each product will embrace a number of technologies. Thus, we really must consider the key technology, which seems to be embryonic in case 1, mature in case 2, probably embryonic in case 3, and in growth stage in case 4.

Figure 7-7 suggests some norms to be associated with each program type. In case 1, emphasis is on program-management and technology strategies. Firms in this category will be trying to move their activities into case 2. The embattled builders of the nuclear power plant, for example, would like to see them more standardized, as fossil-fuel plants are. It is more likely, however, that they would move toward case 3—for example, a gas pipeline following on from the oil pipeline. In case 3 we continue to find emphasis on program-management and technology strategies. We believe firms working in case 3 situations will be trying to move their activities into case 4. Evidence for this can be seen in the struggles of NASA to keep the space program alive. Participants in case 4 emphasize program management and technology. There have been occasional attempts to move some of these businesses into case 2—for example, with an all-purpose standard fighter aircraft—but continually advancing technology and differentiated mission requirements have kept most activity in case 4. It appears advantageous for successful firms to stay there. Finally, those in case 2 will be trying to consolidate their industry, using efficiency strategies and with an emphasis on maintaining or improving competitive position.

Planning for Uncertainty in Large Projects

Karl M. Wiig

In projects that are controlled and affected by chains of events within the implementing organization—chains of events that are caused by other interested parties and by the external environment—there are many uncertainties regarding the costs, schedules, and implications of the project's implementation. There are broad uncertainties during the conceptual stages, and many uncertainties still remain during the planning stages. Although careful planning, studies, and engineering will have eliminated most of the uncertainties, some do last through the project's construction stages. Even at the time of implementation, there are still uncertainties regarding the performance of the project once it has been placed into operation. Some of the uncertainties deal with aspects of the project that may be under the control of the implementing organization; other uncertainties are associated with the adverse or desirable actions by other interested parties who may stand to gain or lose by the implementation of the project; and some are associated with the external environment. The latter category often includes those uncertainties that are associated with regulations, the general behavior of the economy, market conditions, technological developments, and many other factors. Typical unknown future conditions deal with factors that may be under the control of the implementing organization, including uncertainties in schedules, costs of implementing the project, its performance once in operation, and so on.

Thus, the manager who is charged with planning and implementing a large project will benefit from planning for such uncertainties and taking advantage of the means available for him to deal logically and efficiently with such planning. Methods to cope with the uncertainties can be identified and characterized. Planning for uncertainty, although it may require resources beyond those that normally are expended during the planning stages, has its rewards.

The major objective of planning for uncertainty is to decide which strategy should be pursued to the organization's greatest advantage, with the realization that future conditions may vary considerably from a particular deterministic scenario and may be outside the control of the project manager. This decision requires (1) determining which strategies are available for implementation of the project, (2) characterizing the uncertainties that must be considered, and (3) projecting the implications of implementing each of the available strategies for all the relevant futures that are expected to obtain. These analyses can be undertaken at several levels of thoroughness, given the resources available to the manager, the manager's inclination and particular decision-making style, and the time available to develop the information necessary for the decision.

The second objective of planning for uncertainty is to develop contingency plans. As the implications of implementing different strategies are analyzed and studied, management obtains insight into the merits of implementing different strategies. Many new strategies and their variants are explored, providing a basis for selecting and choosing conditional strategies that may involve the same initial stages as the best strategy but contain alternatives for changing the downstream direction of the project as future conditions develop, The objective is to identify robust strategies that permit modification of the project to counter changing future conditions and give the best performance according to the organization's goals over as broad a range of future conditions as possible.

Planning for Uncertainty

In planning for uncertainty, the main objective is to select the strategy that will perform best and to the organization's greatest advantage under the variety of conditions that may be encountered. To perform this selection as an informed decision maker, a number of aspects of the problem must be clarified and investigated to allow proper decision making. The major methodology that is suitable for this type of uncertainty planning is based on the body of knowledge developed for decision making under uncertainty.[1] In general, this process builds on the notion that the following analytical steps can be undertaken logically and rationally:

1. Identify and specify the strategic options that are available to undertake and implement the project. In particular, this step deals with isolating and characterizing, in sufficient detail, the major alternatives or approaches available to implement or complete the project.
2. For each of the strategic alternatives, determine project specifics in terms of the major project activities and their interrelations; the potential schedules and duration of the activities; costs and other resources required to complete activities; decision options that are open to management to change the direction of the project as future conditions vary from those expected; and, for more detailed analyses, many specific functional mechanisms.

3. Determine which uncertainties exist with regard to events that are internal to the implementing organization; events that may be under control of other interested parties; and events that are caused by external and impartial sources.
4. By performing a venture analysis, analyze the implications of undertaking each of the identified strategic options with regard to their acceptability in their support of the organizational objectives.

Planning for uncertainty typically is an iterative process, which requires a repeated refinement of the characterization of the strategic options that are available, the project specifics, and the uncertainties to allow better analysis of their relative preference. Additional benefits are also derived from analysis of the refinement of the project specifics for each strategic option and the associated decision options for coping with future conditions. During this analysis, it becomes necessary to reflect efficient management of the project. Efficient management will appropriately reflect the flexibility and decisions that are available to management to change the project course in order to take advantage of beneficial futures or to counter adverse futures as they appear. As this planning proceeds, more robust plans and variants of the strategic options are developed, providing a basis for developing contingency plans. This type of analysis also provides clear quantitative measures of benefits associated with the costs required to initiate redundant contingency plans early in the project cycle.

Approaches to Support Planning for Uncertainties

Three quantitative approaches to support planning for uncertainties yield explicit information on the advantages and disadvantages of particular strategies: (1) deterministic analysis under multiple scenarios; (2) project evaluation and review technique (PERT); and (3) stochastic project simulation (using Monte Carlo simulation). Other less quantitative approaches can also be pursued, but they are of lesser value to the discriminating decision maker.

Deterministic Analysis under Multiple Scenarios

This approach involves performing the project analysis and project planning that is required during the conceptual stages and later, during the planning and detailed design stages of the project, under several different scenarios that represent the ranges of future conditions as they reasonably may be expected. The steps this analysis normally goes through are as follows:

1. Determine several representative scenarios of future conditions, with specific information on potential schedules, potential costs and resource requirements, expectations for operations, expectations for market conditions, and expectations with regard to external events, such as regulations, economic conditions, and other relevant parameters.
2. Specify the strategic options that are available to undertake and complete the project.
3. Determine the project specifics for each strategy in terms of activities, expected costs, and other relevant items.
4. Analyze the project performance for each strategy and scenario combination.
5. Select the desired strategy to be pursued.

Typically, from four to eight scenarios should be chosen for this type of analysis in order to provide an understanding of how well it may be expected that the different strategies will perform under the variety of future conditions that may be encountered. Ideally, a large number of scenarios should be selected, but this is impractical with this approach. The analysis is normally performed using deterministic manual or computer-based analysis to estimate the explicit performance of each strategy for each scenario.

The advantages of this approach are, first, that the approach is conceptually manageable and requires standard analysis methodologies that often are identical to those used by the organization for other puposes. In addition, the analysis is relatively inexpensive and quick. Analysis using this approach also gives a better perspective and understanding of the performance of different strategies under future conditions than a deterministic (single-scenario) analysis does. Finally, the approach allows, when desired, extremely detailed analysis of a project for each of the discrete scenarios.

The disadvantages of this approach are, first, that its discrete scenarios are representative of only a very small region of future conditions. It is difficult to establish the relative likelihood of occurrence of each scenario and therefore to assess risk expectations appropriately.

The analysis does not readily allow for analysis of "efficient management" of projects since future conditions may vary broadly and since such broad variations from the stated scenario cannot easily be reflected by the methodology.

This approach is relatively common and quite useful under conditions where time is of the essence and there might be other significant restraints which prevent further detailed analysis. The approach is a further elaboration of "sensitivity analysis." Sensitivity analysis, unfortunately, is often implemented as a somewhat arbitrary attempt at creating scenarios which reflect expected deviations in future conditions.

Program Evaluation and Review Technique (PERT)

A well-known and proved technique for examining the effects of duration uncertainties on project completion,[2] PERT allows the use of standard computer-based models that are widely available, but it does not provide a broad and good overview of implications of general uncertainties on the project. In most implementations, PERT programs allow analysis only of project schedules resulting from uncertainties in durations of individual activities. The programs are well designed and generally available, which provides easy access to the methodology by many analysts.

The steps required to perform PERT analysis follow the general pattern of analysis under certainty:

1. Establish and characterize the strategic alternatives that are available to implement the project.
2. Determine activities, precedence relations, durations, and costs for each strategy, and determine specific durations in terms of their low, expected, and high values to characterize the uncertainties for each of the strategic alternatives under consideration.
3. Evaluate the performance of each strategy by building a computer-based PERT network for each strategy, and perform the project-schedule simulation.
4. Select the best strategy in terms of its cost, resource requirements, overall duration, and other organizational objectives.

The steps required to undertake PERT analysis constitute a relatively concise, efficient, and quick program, with moderate expenditure of effort. Its advantages are that it can be used with widely available, easy-to-use, and well-established computer programs. In addition, the approach provides quick, low-cost analysis of uncertainties, with particular emphasis on critical path and project duration. Finally, it provides excellent estimates of project and activity schedules and of other resource requirements (although, in most instances, these are represented by deterministic estimates).

The disadvantages of the PERT approach are that it requires separate network and separate computer models for each alternative strategy. Furthermore, the approach primarily addresses schedule uncertainties and does not allow for comprehensive representation of complex mechanisms within projects, except activity durations and resource estimates. Another disadvantage is that the approach does not allow for decision branching as future conditions change. Finally, it requires very detailed representation of project alternatives.

The PERT approach provides a limited level of understanding of the effects of uncertainties. Since the emphasis of the methodology is to provide insight into schedule changes as a result of uncertainties in durations of individual activities, other insights are not readily obtained. Therefore, it is difficult to use this technique to develop contingency plans and to generate and design more efficient strategies and gain insight into specific aspects of the overall project that are affected by different types of uncertainties.

Stochastic Project Simulation

Stochastic simulation for analyzing complex, large projects has been used regularly for about twenty years by advanced planners in large firms, financial institutions, academia, and governments.[3] Stochastic simulation of the project is performed using Monte Carlo simulation techniques. Uncertain variables and parameters are represented by their probability distributions, and different Monte Carlo scenarios are created by random sampling of these distributions. When many Monte Carlo scenarios (in the hundreds or thousands) are simulated, the project's potential performance can be calculated for a large number of future conditions. When the project is analyzed under uncertainty, the efficient management of the project must be incorporated appropriately and explicitly.

In general, stochastic simulation of a project on a computer requires explicit representation of the following aspects of a project:

1. A model must be developed of the project evolution from the beginning to the end of the planning horizon of interest. This model is often deterministic. It is basically an engineering model (as opposed to an econometric or other statistically structured model). As an engineering model, all the relevant, known mechanisms that relate performance (output) variables with the exogenous (input) variables (often through many intermediate variables) must be explicitly represented, with all their nonlinearities and conditionalities (such as efficient management-decision behavior). Known and uncertain parameters are explicitly included. Since the model must faithfully represent the operation and performance of the project under a wide range of operating and exogenous conditions, mechanisms must be explicitly represented. For a physical project, appropriate mechanisms may include such relations as those between task-

completion time, costs of completing tasks, operating costs of completing tasks, operating-cost revenues, financial operations (loans drawn down and repayments), and annual tax calculations.

2. Calculation methods must be represented for estimating the performance of the project in terms of the desired project operation when the output variables are calculated through simulation.

3. Estimates must be given for all model input parameters and variables, both those that will be represented by deterministic (point) estimates and those whose uncertainty requires that they be represented by probability distributions.

4. Decision options must be given that are open to the implementations of the project regarding project-management aspects and project options (such as a production platform or an undersea system for a second development stage of an offshore oilfield).

The steps that must be followed in a stochastic project simulation are as follows:

1. Specify and characterize main strategic options.
2. Identify and make explicit the uncertainties (internal, other interested parties, external) and the decision options that are available to project management to counteract or take advantage of varying conditions.
3. Construct a computer-based model of the project to incorporate an activity network; a decision tree; complex project mechanisms, such as tax laws, physical phenomena, and partnership agreements; and a project evaluation in terms of costs, benefits, tax, production and related to corporate objectives.
4. By the use of stochastic simulation, evaluate the performance of strategic alternatives under a broad set of future conditions.
5. Develop and evaluate new alternatives and variants of alternatives as additional knowledge is obtained regarding uncertainties, as new ways are found for counteracting uncertainties, and as other aspects of implementing the project are identified.
6. Select the desired strategy and contingency program and evaluate the efficacies of various contingency programs.

Stochastic project simulation normally provides a much better understanding and insight than is possible with most other approaches. It requires significantly more resources, however, and is therefore used primarily to analyze larger projects, which can benefit from such increased expenditures.

The major advantages of stochastic project simulation are, first, that the approach promotes explication of uncertainties and decisions to counter future conditions. It gives excellent insights into implications of uncertainties for each strategic option. It also allows detailed analysis of the project. In addition, this approach provides an efficient framework for developing and analyzing new strategies and variants of proposed strategies. It also supports selection of strategies based on desired posture and trade-offs among objectives, as stated by the supporting organization.

The disadvantages of this approach are, first, that it requires unique computer modeling of projects, which is often time-consuming and costly to implement. In addition, the total analysis is costlier and more time-consuming than other conventional analysis methodologies. Stochastic project simulation requires a high level of expertise to perform and interpret, and it may give wrong insights if it is handled inexpertly. Finally, this approach requires managerial involvement. Although the requirement for managerial involvement is mentioned as a disadvantage, in many instances this feature may become a positive aspect, in that it often provides the decision maker with a much greater involvement and understanding of the problem than other methodologies do.

As an example of stochastic project simulation, consider the total development program for a large oil and gas field in the North Sea. This project has a total capital investment of approximately $5 billion, with several stages and an implementation period of about twelve years. Significant uncertainties exist even after it has been established that the oil and gas resources are of high commercial value. A large number of development strategies may be considered initially, differing in terms of schedules, sizes and location of equipment to be placed in the field, and the technology to be used at each stage. There is considerable flexibility for adjusting the evolution of the project as uncertainties are resolved, but a number of early decisions are almost irreversible: (1) the technology used for the first production platform; (2) the actual placement of the production platform above the geological structure; and (3) the capability of the platform and transportation system. It is therefore very valuable to investigate explicitly how the different implementation strategies are expected to work under the variety of conditions that can be expected for everything from production schedules, implementation cost, and weather conditions to regulatory conditions and market conditions for both oil and gas. The field is situated in the North Sea, approximately 200 miles from the nearest coastline, in waters approximately 100 meters deep. From the initial exploration information, it is expected that the first production will consist only of oil, with full reinjection of the gas until a gas pipeline can be built and used to transport gas to shore. Oil will first be produced through a single-buoy mooring (SBM) system, and this will be replaced at a later stage by an oil pipeline to shore. Two development stages are envisioned. In the first stage, a combined drilling and production-housing platform (Condeep design) will be installed. The second stage will consist of either installation of a second drilling and production-housing Condeep platform or installation of a new technology—underwater completion system. Thus, there are a large number of options regarding the capacity of these objects, the schedule of their implementation, and their actual physical location.

Generally, the explicit use of the information that will be obtained from planning for uncertainty in this project is required during several stages of the planning process to support decisions and further planning. The planning process is indicated in figure 8–1. The particular points at which formal analysis is performed are as follows:

1. Concept development,[4] relatively early in the planning cycle, when many concepts are identified and considered;
2. Concept selection, when one or two major concepts are chosen to be engineered and planned further, at which stage there are still a number of variants for each major concept;
3. Specification and engineering of the development strategy, when one major concept has been finally selected and variants of that concept are explored, some being considered directly for implementation, others being identified as contingency plans;
4. Selection of the particular concept variant to be provided for commercialization and implementation, when contingency plans for this concept development are also prepared.

The example we are examining is a stochastic project simulation at the first stage of the planning process—concept development. The computer-based model and the associated data bases were designed very comprehensively to support planning analysis at all four decision points throughout the planning process. Planning for uncertainties in such a project has several objectives. Early in the planning process, the major objective is to assist in developing and analyzing project-implementation strategies. Later in the planning process, probabilistic information must be developed to provide a basis for corporate production and revenue forecasts, and capital requirements. Since oil production around the North Sea involves the development and production of a publicly owned resource, the probabilistic information is also required to develop reliable and insightful information about the future for communication to governments and the public in addition to communication within the firm.

Analysis Approach. To perform a stochastic project simulation, a number of strategic options to be analyzed were identified for seven life-cycle stages of the field: exploration; Stage 1 development; initial transportation program; initial operation; Stage 2 development; Stage 2 operations; and field shutdown. Two of these strategic options are shown in simplified form in

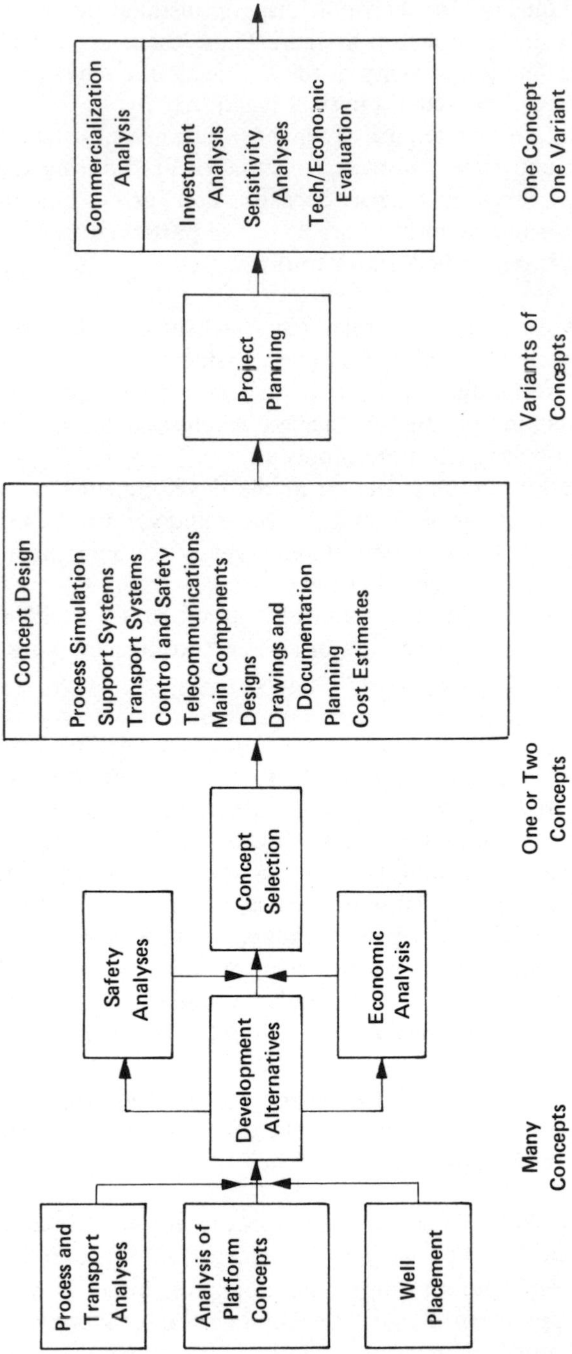

Figure 8–1. Planning Process

Table 8-1
Example Strategies

	Planned Completion Date
Project Strategy 4	
Build first Condeep platform	
(medium processing cap)	1986
Build oil pipeline to shore	1986
Build gas pipeline to shore	1989
Expand field with second Condeep platform	1991
Project Strategy 7	
Build first Condeep platform	
(large processing cap)	1985
Produce from single-buoy mooring	1985
Build gas pipeline	1988
Build oil pipeline	1988
Expand field with underwater completion systems	1990

table 8-1. The strategies were identified in terms of the major objects to be built and implemented (for example, platform or pipeline), their schedule of implementation, their capacity, and their physical placement.

The major uncertainties in this example project are those associated with the amount, physical location, and composition of the available oil and gas deposits. The secondary uncertainties deal with achievable final implementation schedules, implementation costs, and such external conditions as weather conditions during construction seasons. Other uncertainties are regulatory decisions (regarding operating practices or requirements for combined housing and production platforms, and the like, market conditions, and accidents. As a result, a number of major decisions can be envisioned to cope with future conditions as they develop throughout the project:

1. Develop the appraised prospect or abandon:
2. Select the Stage 1 development concept;
3. Select oil-transport systems;
4. Expedite, slow down, or proceed as planned on schedule for Platform 1;
5. Develop stage 2 or stop development with Stage 1;
6. Select the Stage 2 concept;
7. Expedite, slow down, or proceed as planned with Stage 2 development;
8. Produce more or shut down the field.

These decisions constitute the major decision points over the life of the project. In addition, a large number of minor actions can be taken.

For the purpose of simulating the individual project strategies as the project evolves over time, a relatively aggregated activity network is designed. This network characterizes the overall project in such a way that all contemplated strategies can be incorporated. A simplified network for this project indicates, in the activities associated with the implementation of the major platform during Phase 1, two concepts for Stage 2 and the installation of a gas pipeline (see figure 8-2). The installation of an oil pipeline is not included in this version of the network.

A detail of the associated project decision tree indicates where the decision points and the uncertainties associated with exploration and the first part of Stage 1 development are (see figure 8-3). The complete decision tree, including all uncertainties, has almost a hundred probability distributions (see figure 8-4). Several of the initial probability distributions are indicated with sample data in table 8-2. Another example of a more detailed approach is used to characterize the uncertainties associated with price

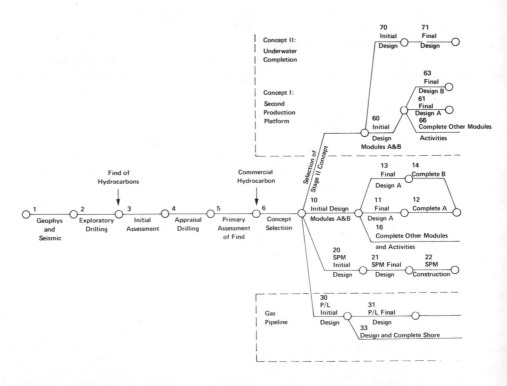

Figure 8-2. Simplified Project Network

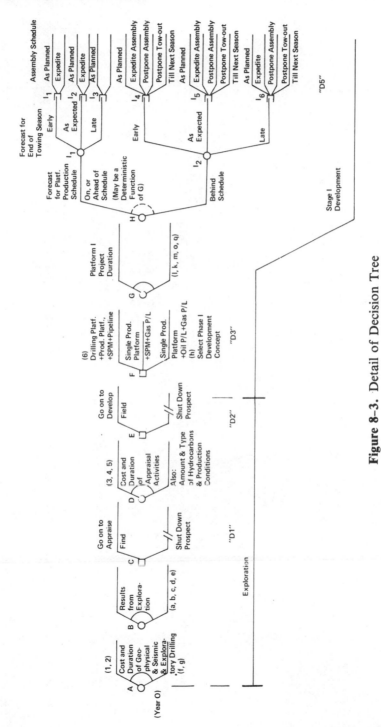

Figure 8-3. Detail of Decision Tree

New Dimensions of Project Management

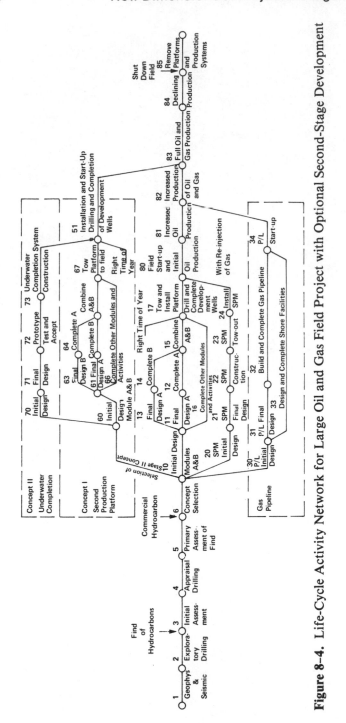

Figure 8-4. Life-Cycle Activity Network for Large Oil and Gas Field Project with Optional Second-Stage Development

Table 8-2
States Associated with Some Example Events for Crude-Oil Price Forecasting

Posted Price in 1981 (1979$)	Political Stability in Middle East	OPEC Price Rise in 1982	Difference in Spot-Market Conditions in 1982 from Posted Prices
$20/bbl	Stable	−10%	10% below posted prices
$24/bbl	Some unrest	0	At posted prices
$30/bbl	Significant unrest with some oil-production interference	10	10% above posted prices
$50/bbl	War	25	25% or more above posted prices

forecasts, including an elaborate submodel for the generation of forecasts on market conditions in target years (see table 8-3).

Results have been developed for two major strategy options pursued for further development from a total of more than twenty-five analyzed strategies (table 8-4). Strategy (4) involves a conventional development program at a relatively secure schedule, whereas strategy (7) involves a slightly accelerated development program using new technology—underwater completion systems. In constructing the mathematical models for the simulation of the project, the implementation-project strategy is simulated for several hundred future scenarios to develop probability distributions for all the main variables to reflect the operations and other strategically important aspects of the project. Some of these variables are the following:

1. Capital investment required by year;
2. Production streams of oil and gas, from different areas of the field and in total;
3. Economic risks (some of which may be insurable);
4. The amount of oil and gas in place and available for recovery;
5. The year for first production obtained from the project in each of the scenarios simulated; and
6. The economic returns in terms of net present value, return on investment, and other indicators.

Two of the actual probability distributions obtained by ordering the information from each scenario are indicated in figure 8-5 for platform

Table 8–3
Probability Distributions that Characterize Uncertainties

	Minimum	Probable	Maximum
Recoverable oil (tons)	200	800	2,100
Depth of payzone (m)	2,300	3,200	5,000
Production ratio of associated gas to oil (mm³ gas/ton oil)	0.2	0.4	1.2
Duration of exploration, activities 1–5 (mo.)	43	52	72
Platform 1 initial design duration for one predetermined concept (mo.)	12	15	18
Platform 1 duration, design and complete modification A (mo.)	12	15	24
Recoverable gas (billion m³)	100	400	1,700
Well productivity (equivalent oil ton/day)	200	800	2,000
Cost of exploration, activities 1–5 ($ millions)	4.5	11.0	21.0
Duration for concept selection (mo.)	19	15	30
Platform 1 initial design cost for one predetermined concept ($ millions)	8	15	18
Platform cost, design and complete modification A ($ millions)	500	750	1,600

Table 8–4
Results for Example Strategies

	Strategy 4	Strategy 7
Completion date (first production by end of year)		
1985	5%	57%
1986	60	86
1987	93	97
1988	98	99
Expected production date	1987	1985
Economic returns		
More than 10% internal rate of return	95%	90%
More than 20% internal rate of return	83	71
More than 30% internal rate of return	2	12
More than 40% internal rate of return	1	2
Expected return (internal rate of return)	23	27

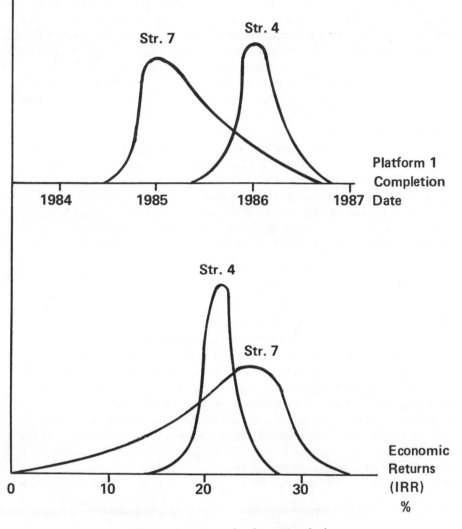

Figure 8–5. Results from Analysis

completion date and internal rate of return (IRR). These probability distributions, shown for Strategies 4 and 7, indicate that the platform completion date to be expected from the two strategies roughly conforms to the intended schedules. For Strategy 7, however, some extreme delays in completing Platform 1 must result because of adverse effects caused by the accelerated implementation program. The economic returns, however, indicate a different set of probability distributions and show that Strategy 7 has, on the average, a larger chance to provide better economic returns than Strategy 4 (27 percent versus 23 percent, as was shown in table 8-4). Strategy 7 also has a significant probability to yield a lower economic return than Strategy 4 will under the worst circumstances, and therefore Strategy 7 is significantly more risky than Strategy 4. By obtaining detailed information on the conditions leading to economic returns for Strategy 7 of less than 20 percent, explicit analysis has been performed to identify how Strategy 7 may be modified to reduce its vulnerability and therefore make it better and more robust.

Many probability distributions and other statistical data are developed for each development strategy. This information provides extensive insight into many aspects of the implementation of the strategies and into the conditions that can cause things to go wrong and must be planned for to be avoided. The information that is developed in many instances shows clearly that particular strategies are indirectly vulnerable and cannot readily be modified and restructured to become desirable and advantageous.

Conclusion

The analysis for the example project required about eight man years. It included identification of project alternatives, characterization of uncertainties, determination of decision options and other data, building and implementation of the mathematical model, development of the data base, and performance of the analysis. These were all in addition to what is normally required for economic and engineering planning for such a project. The level of effort is typical for the detailed examination of such projects and therefore constitutes a significant allocation of resources to answer the planning questions that are posed. The majority of this effort came from the corporation's own engineering and planning groups, rather than from outside sources. In the process, the corporation's staff were developing an extensive understanding and insight into the available implementation strategies and their variants. The process provided significant involvement of management at several different levels of the organization to identify and engineer new strategic outcomes. As a result, the process provided a deep general understanding of the options that were available to pursue the implementation of the project, its implications, and how the options could be modified to meet different future conditions. The process also resulted in deliberate engineering of better strategic options and of the variants of strategic options that could provide bases for contingency plans.

The major benefits provided by planning for uncertainty are that different strategic options can be compared over a large range and number of

Table 8–5
Some Benefits of Planning for Uncertainty

Cost of thorough analysis	$100,000 to $500,000
Differences in expectations for strategies (for $2 billion project)	$100 million to $300 million net present value
Improvement in expectations for good strategies as a result of refined what-if analysis	$10 million to $50 million net present value
Matched selection of strategy with desired risk posture	
Identification of uncertainties and design strategies that can cope with them	

future conditions and that representative statistics are developed to allow explicit comparative analysis (see table 8–5). For a $2 billion project, differences in what were thought to be similarly attractive strategies ranged up to $300 million (in expected net present value). This type of analysis thus provides an entirely different foundation and insight for basing selection of the strategies. It also allows direct inclusion of the corporation's desired risk posture in the selection process.

The next major benefit of comprehensive planning for uncertainty is the framework it provides for developing better variants of good strategies and for identifying good contingency strategies and plans. As the framework is used for what-if analysis, new project variants are developed to improve the economic expectations by up to $50 million.

Additional benefits are derived from the perspective that this type of analysis provides management. When the implementation implications of a broad range of future conditions are examined, unpleasant surprises are reduced and a better understanding is developed of why a project does not proceed according to plan. The major advantage of this understanding often is that management is also prepared to consider how the new conditions should be dealt with and what the best project strategies are from a given point onward. Thus, planning for uncertainties puts management in a position to select a better plan and to take corrective actions better and earlier.

Notes

1. H. Raiffa, *Decision Analysis: Introductory Lectures* (Reading, Mass.: Addison-Wesley, 1968); R.O. Schlaifer, *Analysis of Decisions Under Uncertainty* (New York: McGraw-Hill, 1969).

2. A good discussion of the PERT approach may be found in F.S. Hiller and G.J. Lieberman, *Operations Research* (San Francisco: Holden-Day, 1974).

3. Discussion of the general methodology can be found in, for example, L.Y. Pouliquen, "Risk Analysis in Project Appraisal," World Bank Staff Occasional Papers #11 (Baltimore, The John Hopkins University Press, 1970); and A.C. Hax and K.M. Wiig, "The Use of Decision Analysis in Capital Investment Problems," *Sloan Management Review* 17 (Winter 1976):19–38.

4. The term *concept* reflects the total development strategy through all stages, including field shutdown.

9 Project Financing

Theodore V. Fowler

Project financing is a key element in the overall project-management function, yet it usually is only tangentially considered in discussing project-management problems. The investment banker, however, has become well versed in the subject through firsthand involvement. Although an investment bank has no money to lend and little or no money to invest, it is in the middle between borrowers and lenders, and it works to arrange financing for projects. Thus it is concerned with the intricacies of project financing—the problem of raising substantial amounts of capital in the real world, with all its bottlenecks.

Today, project financing is not as easy as it apparently used to be. Therefore, those who are putting projects together today must include finance early in the planning function. A discussion of some actual project circumstances and how the financial transactions actually occurred are the best way to prove my point. On New Year's Eve 1979, we (The First Boston Corporation, New York) were called by a Dutch company that had just posted a $20 million performance bond on an $800+ million gas-pipeline project in Argentina. It had done all the engineering and had bid for an operating concession on a lump-sum, fixed-price, date-certain basis. The bond required that the company let pipe orders out within sixty days of the date of contract award. When the company was notified that it had won the bid, it then realized that it had not yet arranged for financing the $800 million—a very substantial capital amount. In effect, we had 60 days to arrange $800 million in true, nonrecourse project financing. (I will discuss later whether or not we succeeded in that mission.)

The point of this example is that financial engineering is now as relevant as basic engineering, planning engineering, and any other type of engineering that is considered in the planning phase of a project. Project financing can be thought of in a systems sense and placed within an overall project-planning, project-management function, but it cannot be thought about out of the context of the real world of money. Current capital markets can be thought of as comprising two sectors: the bank sector worldwide and the institutional sector, predominantly in the United States. Those very important sources of money are considering some very important changes in the way they will make their funds available to projects.

First, banks are being forced to look at projects aggressively because they are under a great deal of competitive pressure. Non-U.S. banks, in particular, are placing a great deal of pressure on U.S. banks. Banks also are under competitive pressure from an alternative capital market—commercial paper—which is now a $150 billion source of funding and is cheaper than bank money—about 200 basis points. Consequently, banks are willing to take greater risks in lending their money and therefore are a much more interesting source of project financing.

Institutions such as life-insurance companies and pension funds are a vast source of money. Even though, nominally, none of the investments they have made over the last ten to fifteen years are in default, they have in fact lost money. Their portfolios are worth fifty to seventy-five cents on the dollar because most of their loans were made at low, fixed rates of interest, during a period when inflation has taken the real world of interest rates to much higher levels. As a result, they are now looking for inflation-hedged investments. Thus, institutions, too, for an entirely different reason than that of the banks, are now willing to take risks in their portfolio investments.

In addition to these motivating factors that are affecting the supply side of project financing, there are new demand-side factors in the project-finance equation. Ten years ago, corporations had very little short-term debt on their balance sheets; overall, long-term debt was at acceptable levels, and industry as a whole had a very solid credit rating. Now, however, corporations sponsoring projects are suffering from a general overall decline in their credit standing. Utility companies are paying dividends on a return-on-capital basis, and major industrial companies are suffering inadequate profitability and have financial ratios that are inadequate to sponsor projects with any guarantee that they will be able to continue to do so until completion. Thus, corporate sponsors are trying to lay off risks in order to catalyze projects.

With money sources that, now more than ever, are willing to take risks and with project sponsors (whether corporations or countries) that are in need of allocating risks, the project-financing environment is conducive to creating a new entity—that is, money lenders that will more readily take certain project risks, provided project sponsors and others inject equity and performance-designated undertakings (short of financial guarantees).

The technology of putting deals together in this new environment is what I call true project financing. In a planning sense, this technology can be ordered early, so that it can generate information that is useful to both the financial engineers and the basic engineers. Project planners must provide the financial engineers with the informational ammunition to get projects financed. A total feasibility-planning effort must include a detailed financing plan.

Project finance, like other areas, uses a great deal of jargon that means different things to different people. Sponsors try to get the debt of projects off their balance sheets in a variety of different ways. Lenders have a different perspective; they look at how much recourse they have to the sponsor. Thus, it is necessary to become comfortable with their accounting and credit jargon. When one cuts through all the jargon, however, one realizes that project finance is not anything magical. It does not substitute for credit; rather, it is a technique for creating credit.

Creating credit is a complicated discipline that is not necessarily capable of dealing with bigness or complexity, although that, too, may be part of the equation. Some people associate project finance only with big projects, but a big project is not necessarily going to be project financed. Consider the Philippines Nuclear Project, which is entirely owned by the Philippine government, which will guarantee the debt of the project. That is not true project financing, because it does not fit the equation in which lenders participate in project risk. By definition, then, bigness alone is not sufficient to warrant project financing. Similarly, some people think that complexity warrants project financing. The Trans Alaskan Pipeline has been called a project; in proper focus, however, it is clear that Exxon, Arco, and Sohio/BP directly financed their respective shares of that project. The project itself did not finance; rather, sponsors financed, pooled their money, and built the project.

How does one structure a project so that lenders look first to its cash flow and only secondarily, and to a limited extent, to its sponsors? Basically, how does one create the building blocks to limit the recourse of project sponsors to some manageable undertakings and still allow a new entity to raise capital? In a system orientation, there are six management steps in pulling together financing for a project.

For a project to go out and borrow on its own, rather than the sponsor's taking care of it, project planners must generate, early, the kind of information that is useful to investment banks, commercial banks, and merchant banks so that they ultimately can raise the money on a feasible and economic basis. Essentially, involving a banker in a feasibility study means working with the capital-cost estimates, production-yield estimates, and operating-cost factors (to name a few) to develop an idea of the maximum amount of money that is going to be needed to finance the project under the worst circumstances. If an attempt is made to raise project capital from sophisticated lenders without sponsor guarantees and the lenders can second-guess your assumptions about capital cost, inflation rates, time to completion, start-up curve, sustained yields, sustained maintenance costs, and the like (that is, all the things inherent to a project's economics), then it will not be possible to raise capital on the basis now being sought by corporate and developing-country sponsors. Thus, in order to think about a project's financing in the early management stages, project planners unfortunately must get involved with the details affecting a project's cash-flow economics and sensitivities thereto.

Having initially addressed feasibility issues, project planners must next turn to structuring projects so that the legal form of the project contributes to its economics. The synfuels industry, for example, is clearly an area in which legal form is important. If a synfuels project is a corporation rather than a partnership, the distinction favors the partnership (because of construction-period tax-credit flow-throughs and interest deductions). A sponsor of a synfuels project, after taxes, can have no net-equity money invested under a proper partnership structure; whereas, if the project is structured as a corporation, the sponsor would have to fund his equity investment pursuant to the drawn-down schedule for equity capital, without any tax relief. The tax, legal, and business structures of projects are thus vital to project economics. If these structures are not planned early enough and if important decisions are naively taken, the project's economics can be severely jeopardized, if not forgone.

Once financial responsibility and structuring are thought through, it is then possible to think about sponsorship, credit, risk allocation, and the financing plan (that is, where money actually may come from).

There may be many rationales for sponsorship participants. Many projects are joint undertakings, such as joint ventures between companies, joint ventures between companies and countries, and joint ventures between individuals, corporate users and takers, multinationals and nationals. All these joint ventures must have one overriding theme, however: the sponsors must come together for the right economic reasons. If one is going to spend many hours working on a project that will never happen because it is not well sponsored, one can know that at the outset—and decline to work on it—by systematically assessing its sponsorship separately from its economics. By asking why a sponsor is involved, one can preempt a negative financing result when the prospective lenders ask the sponsor to assume certain project risks. If that sponsor is not involved for the right reasons, no matter how one plans the project and no matter how good it may look economically, the sponsor is not going to go forward. Hence, project planners, in addition to being acutely aware of economic feasibility, must be extremely careful and extremely cynical about sponsorship at an early stage. Otherwise, a great deal of study money will get spent and a great deal of time will be wasted on projects that will not proceed.

Basis for credit is the next thing to examine. Can the project raise money in whole or in part on its own (that is, to what extent do sponsors or third parties need to provide support mechanisms for the borrowing)? Once one asks that question, one can start looking at the basics of how to finance the project. The only way to come to a decision that the project is financeable on its own is to be able to make an assessment that a lender (who views himself as a renter of money) will perceive that he can get his money back from the project in all events. To the extent that there are issues in sponsorship or economics that are not manageable lender risks, one then must begin what amounts to a risk-allocation process.

Again, if project planners are going to produce feasible projects, they must develop, early, business arrangements between and among all parties of interest in the project, which will have the effect of apportioning the various risks in a project to designated parties—including, when possible, to lenders. Since lenders now are willing to take much more risk than they might have three or four years ago, project managers now are in the position of determining whether a project is going to happen. When a project is marginal, creative financing can make the difference. Thus, engaging a financial engineer is just as important as engaging a basic engineer.

Conceptually, project planning of risk allocation can be very simple; one is trying to give lenders the perception that, in all events, there will be cash flow to repay project loans. The engineer and everybody involved must keep their minds on this simple cash-flow orientation, because it is the key to raising project capital. Project planners are trying to cope with three kinds of risks to the satisfaction of lenders: completion risks, operating risks, and such other risks as regulatory risk. If one is trying to get away from financing at the sponsor level to finance at the project level, one has to cover all three of these risk areas to the satisfaction of a lender. Financial engineers do this through an almost infinite variety of contractual agreements, each of which can serve many purposes.

What do we mean by completion risks? If the project planner is going to try to raise project capital without a guarantee, he must question whether he can get the project built on time and, if not, what the cash flow sensitivity to a time delay is. How much does a month's delay cost the project? Can it be built for projected cost? Related questions involve whether the inflation assumption is correct; what if the probability of design error is such that the planner might have to go back and start all over halfway through the process; and what the probability is of work stoppage or a major unforeseen event that will inhibit completion. Finally, it is not enough just to install that last bolt; one has to ask, also whether the project is going to work to design specification.

Although financial intermediaries find it desirable to stay away from sponsor guarantees of project debt during the construction period, guaranteeing debt during construction is different from guaranteeing debt during the life of a project. In essence, the planning phase of a project involves figuring out which party of interest will take which project risk. More and more construction companies that want business, for example, are entering into very performance-oriented terms of contracting for projects. As a result, a third-party project-procurement contract can sometimes be used by sponsors as a device for absorbing completion risks to the satisfaction of the lender. Thus, in addition to the owner and the lender, it is possible to introduce the contractor, the vendor, and the supplier of products or equipment into a position of absorbing selected project risks. In a corn-derived ethanol project, for example, wherein the contractor has entered into a lump-sum, date-certain, fixed-price contract that provides for a guaranteed minimum yield with liquidated damage clauses, a lender sees that, although the owner is not taking the completion risk, neither is the lender. Thus, he will be assigned a strong contract from a bona fide contractor that will assume a substantial portion of the perceived completion risk.

When project planning is completed and the project is through its initial start-up phase, it enters the operating phase, in which there are many operating risks that might result in interruption of cash flow. The project-planning task is to identify those factors in advance and figure out which party of interest will risk some of the prospective defaults that may occur during the operating period. Looking at the problem systematically, there are three classes of interested parties that could take these risks: owners (preferably not), users, and takers, or third parties. These parties can work either together or in different roles. Owners can enter into cash-deficiency agreements (or many similar contracts), which basically claim that, if there is a cash shortfall, it will be covered by the sponsor. These contracts can be limited in dollar amounts; they can be limited in time; or they can fall away once performance levels have been reached. Although project planners may think these are merely details, Exxon, Arco, and some of the other credit-worthy corporate sponsors often regard such details as critical to project feasibility. Without an early start in defining some method of integrating the owner into the credit-support scheme, the project planner will not have a project. One must define the owners' commitment to the project as part of the early thinking about project feasibility. Commitment can take the form of equity, cash-support agreements, product-purchase agreements, and the like, all of which will lead the lender to perceive adequate sponsorship by the owner.

Users can support a project by many different types of contracts. They can be users in the sense that they will contract to use the facility, such as tolling their bauxite through an alumina plant. Every industry has a unique business method of determining economics roles. As a result, there are several different ways to integrate users with sponsors into the overall credit support of a project. The project user is thus another party that can be part of the process of building credit.

Finally, project managers, project advisors to countries, project consultants, contractors, and bankers must consider the techniques of integrating third parties into the credit structure of project financing. If a project is not

properly planned and structured, for example, it will lose access to the con-
cessionary export-credit sources that are now so attractive. If project planners do not think about procurement mechanics early in the planning process and get too far down the path of procuring equipment, they can lose
access to export-credit dollar-based financing (now at 8.5 percent on a long-
term basis), and such financing may be the key to the economics of the project. Thus, project planners must relate financing to procurement and must
do it in the right sequence. The end result, if it is done right, will be that the
French, the Germans, the Japanese, and any one of several other governmental agencies could assume a great deal of project risk through their con-
cessionary export-credit programs. If procurement is mismanaged or handled in the wrong sequence, the project will lose the possibility of allocating
project risks to this third-party group.

As another example, the best potential new project source now is the
Synthetic Fuels Corporation (SFC). To the extent that the SFC survives
with a meaningful mandate, if project planners do not think it through correctly, they will cause the project to miss the sole basis on which many synfuel and alternative-energy projects might be consummated. It is interesting
that, even before they have a project-financing plan, companies are filing
requests for financing from the SFC because of its perceived impact on
project feasibility.

As final examples of third-party risk allocation, many multilateral
agencies, such as the World Bank and the Inter-American Development
Bank, have programs that are potential sources of credit or capital. In addition, commercial-bank letters of credit, both trade and financial, are excellent means of allocating risk away from sponsors. Some use letters of credit,
for example, to backstop foreign projects so that they can have access to
U.S. capital markets. Finally, third-party coverage of political risk or major
unforeseen risk can be purchased from insurers of business risk, again to
the satisfaction of lenders.

Each of these risk-allocation concepts is entirely different from the
others. Taken collectively, however, if project planners do not consider
them soon enough, they may foreclose the opportunity to feasibly finance
the project. Thus, financing will become the bottleneck because, currently,
even the U.S. government is having difficulty meeting its borrowing needs.
In this type of capital-market environment, it thus becomes critical to focus
systematically on the detailed elements that will affect the project financing
of new project entities.

In summary, financing has become a most critical issue relating to project feasibility. I have set forth a systematic way of organizing the project-
planning process so that it includes an orderly approach to financial engineering. The financial-engineering system that can be successfully implemented focuses on critical repeating issues that affect project economics

and, hence, project finance feasibility. Because project sponsors cannot, and will not, absorb all project risks and because other parties of interest to a project (including lenders) are willing, for their respective reasons, to share in the project risk-allocation process, this system leads to a financial plan that capitalizes importantly on the following:

1. The rationale for a sponsor's project participation;
2. The inherent economics of the project itself;
3. The contribution to economics that a suitable legal, business, tax, and accounting project structure can afford;
4. The basis for credit on which the project will finance; and
5. The allocation of project risk that evolves from the convergence of the foregoing four issues.

The final issue, successful project-finance implementation, is obviously the end result of systematic project planning.

Earlier in this chapter, I promised to discuss how the Dutch company in my example finally achieved the $800 million financing for the Argentine gas-pipeline project concession they had won. They had become totally bottlenecked by financing—to the point where availability of money was almost more important than the terms by which it could be obtained. Bearing in mind that the Dutch company was not willing to provide a sponsor guarantee of project indebtedness, the following miracle was achieved. Regarding equipment procurement, it was determined that a competitive procurement strategy was the key to financing. Within several weeks, a solicitation was made to two countries, asking them to bid for the pipe and equipment on an all-or-none basis—with full financing to be provided. Two positive responses were received, and negotiations were conducted essentially on the basis of price. Regarding local content and interest during construction; The balance of financing was arranged through a syndicate of banks, on the basis of an approximate 50 percent guarantee by an insurance program offered by the winning-country bidder. What sponsor credit support did the Dutch provide? Insofar as the $800 million included construction-period progress profits, such profits were setoff in a cost-overrun completion fund, which, though a finite capital pool, was perceived by lenders to be sufficient coverage of completion risk. Regarding the operating period, lenders were assigned a throughput tariff that required the Argentine government to pay a minimum bill for service—provided the pipeline was first complete and available for service; this was a user credit support. Finally, the aforementioned insurance policy covered, to a limited extent, certain other project risks; this was third-party credit support. The result was that this package of credit support, though not full credit support, was perceived to be sufficient by the various lenders, and the project proceeded on schedule.

Although this transaction may seem very simple, 800 million of any-thing is a great deal—particularly when it must be secured within six weeks. A better and earlier project-planning function might have made it possible to finance this project with much less pressure.

Part IV
Project Control and
Risk Management

10 Assessment and Management of International Project Risk

Stephen W. Ritterbush

Two trends that converged during the 1970s altered the international project environment and significantly increased the risks associated with project management and control. One trend was the result of far-reaching changes in the international economic scene; the other resulted from changes in the size and complexity of projects being undertaken overseas, particularly in the developing world.

Following the initial round of OPEC price increases in 1973–1974, a massive transfer of wealth occurred between the oil-importing nations of the world and the oil-producing nations. In the four years immediately following the OPEC embargo in 1973, the annual surplus of funds amassed by the OPEC nations ranged between $30 billion and $60 billion per year (see figure 10–1). Both the industrialized and the developing world were forced to dig deep to pay for their oil imports, but the outlay was particularly hard on the non-oil-producing, less-developed countries.

By 1978, these surpluses had virtually disappeared, largely because there was both a general decline in worldwide oil consumption and a reverse transfer of wealth between the oil-producing and non-oil-producing nations, which was orchestrated through the international banking community. The large imbalance in the international financial system, however, returned with a vengence immediately thereafter, as a result of the largest oil-price increases in history, between December 1978 and March 1980. OPEC's doubling of the price of a barrel of oil from $18 to more than $36 generated a surplus of more than $65 million on the OPEC countries' accounts in 1979. It is now around $100 billion. These days, however, the world monetary system is far less well equipped to deal with the OPEC surplus than it was immediately following the 1973 embargo.

During the first series of price increases in the mid-1970s, a large proportion of the surplus accumulated by the oil-exporting nations was invested in the major international banks of Europe, Japan, and the United States. The banks, in turn, used these deposits to finance and expand their own loan portfolios. It soon became apparent that, although a great deal of this money was financing projects in the industrialized nations, a large proportion of this transfer was being used as commercial loans to support infrastructure projects in developing countries in Africa, Asia, and South America.

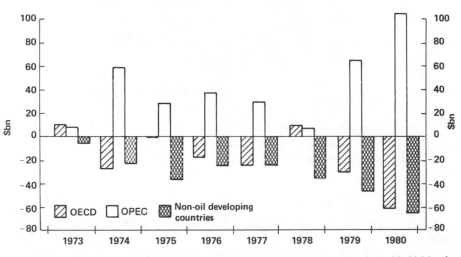

Source: "International Banking Survey," *The Economist Newspaper* (London), 22–28 March 1980. Reprinted with permission.

Figure 10–1. Current-Account Balances of Major World Groupings

Partly because of the need to recycle OPEC deposits, the largest European and U.S. banking corporations rapidly expanded their operations and loan portfolios throughout the developing world during the early to mid-1970s. A good example of this trend is the fact that the international earnings of the thirteen largest banking corporations in the United States increased nearly tenfold between 1970 and 1979 to nearly $1 billion. By the end of the decade, their percentages of earnings from their domestic and international operations were essentially equal (see figure 10–2).

For the developing world, caught between rising oil prices and the needs of their economic-development programs, monetary transfers in the form of commercial loans were a mixed blessing. The pace of economic development has been brought to a virtual standstill in recent years as monies that were once earmarked for this purpose have been diverted to pay for oil imports. In many developing countries, it is not uncommon for 25 percent to 35 percent of total foreign-exchange earnings to be used to pay for oil. Every time the price of oil rises by one dollar per barrel, the World Bank estimates that the non-oil-producing developing countries have to find nearly $2 billion more per year to pay for their oil-import needs.

Because of the sheer size of their financing need to pay for oil imports as well as to support economic development, many of the non-oil-producing less-developed countries have ceased to be aid recipients and, instead, have become commercial borrowers. In 1970, only 17 percent of the debt in the

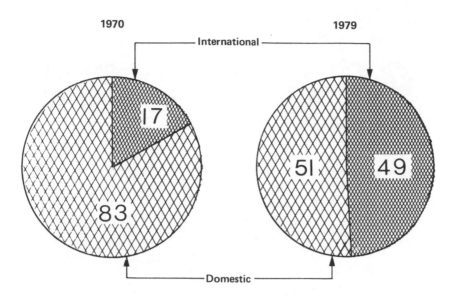

Figure 10–2. Domestic and International Percentages of Total Earnings of Major U.S. Banks

less-developed world was to commercial lenders. By the end of the decade, commercial loans comprised more than 38 percent of all outstanding debt (see figure 10–3). Moreover, the drive to maintain economic growth at pre-1973 levels while paying for oil imports at postembargo prices increased the total debt of these countries from $75 billion to $355 billion during this same period—enough to run the state of Massachusetts for the next fifty years.

As the importance of commercial borrowing has increased among the developing nations in recent years, so has the cost of servicing this debt. Interest and repayment of capital among these nations was 12.5 percent of total debt in 1970. By 1975, this figure had risen to nearly 17 percent, and it is probably even higher today as a result of the significant rise in commercial interest rates during the past year.

During the 1980s, it is unlikely that the oil-importing nations of the world will resolve the conflicts they currently face on the international financial scene. This is particularly true in the case of the world's less-developed countries, which can be expected to bear the costs of a large proportion of the OPEC surplus for some time to come. The projected current-account deficit for the non-oil-producing developing countries is now greater than $60 billion. This figure will only get worse before it gets better.

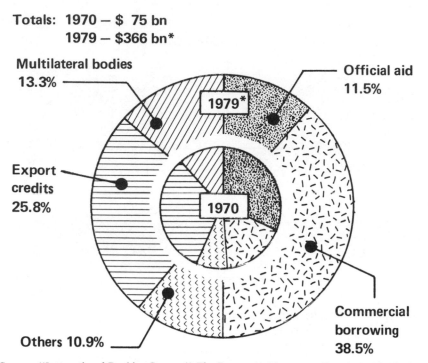

Totals: 1970 — $ 75 bn
        1979 — $366 bn*

Multilateral bodies
13.3%

Official aid
11.5%

1979*

Export
credits
25.8%

1970

Commercial
borrowing
38.5%

Others 10.9%

Source: "International Banking Survey," *The Economist Newspaper* (London), 22–28 March 1980. Reprinted with permission.

Figure 10-3. Less-Developed Countries, Outstanding Debt, by Type of Lender

One may ask what these trends have to do with the international project environment in the years ahead. First, even given the present state of international economic affairs, the pace of construction of large-infrastructure projects throughout the world will not slow to a great degree. Any project that is even remotely able to reduce the less-developed countries' rate of oil consumption—hydroelectric projects, for example—will certainly be given high priority. For the host country or project owner, however, they will become more expensive. Access to capital will become a critical factor in determining which projects are implemented. If the non-oil-producing nations of Asia, Africa, and South America are to sustain a reasonable rate of economic growth in the coming years, the World Bank estimates that their net capital needs will grow during the coming decade to more than $184 billion by 1990. Removing inflationary trends from these figures, it appears that these countries will require a net capital increase of about 4 percent a year. In the coming decade, the world's commercial-banking community could provide as much as half of this total figure. If this course were followed, the dcbt-service liabilities of the less-developed countries would increase accordingly, as many governments would be forced to pay heavier charges for their shorter-term commercial debt. These trends are combining to increase the already precarious economic position of many developing countries. By the end of the 1970s, several countries came perilously close to national bankruptcy. The coming years are almost certain to bring more to that point.

Considering this, the financial and management risks of working abroad, particularly in the developing world, will certainly increase further in the near future. If these risks are combined with the fact that many international projects have become increasingly larger and more sophisticated—a second major trend that began during the 1970s—it becomes obvious that the broad range of risks associated with the international project environment is expanding and is likely to become even more complex during the 1980s (see table 10-1).

On any major project, domestic or international, there are three main objectives: to complete the project at or under cost, to complete it within the specified contract time period, and to complete it to the scope called for in the contract. The more effort that is devoted to identifying and minimizing the risks that accompany each stage of a project from its initial conceptualization and feasibility stages through its actual construction, the easier it is to meet these three objectives. Because of the increasing size and complexity of international projects and the growing number of uncertainties in the international economic environment, as much attention will have to be devoted to the front-end analysis of assessing the risks associated with a project as has been paid to the management of the implementation stages of a project.

Most approaches that are used to identify and assess the risks associated with a project focus primarily on factors in the country's business environment, including the overall political climate, the economic situation, and various social and cultural factors. Although these approaches may meet the needs of the major international banks or a multinational corporation in assessing a country in terms of its political or broad economic risk, they only provide a general overview and in most cases do not fulfill the needs of the constructor-owner, which must deal with the country's institutions on a more intimate level. Any project, no matter where it is undertaken, will be affected by two very different but interrelated environments: the country environment and the project environment.

To understand how these environments are related, it might be best to visualize them as a series of concentric spheres (see figure 10-4). The center or focal point is the actual project. Surrounding the project is the project

Table 10-1
Large International Projects and Approximate Costs
(billions of dollars)

Project	Cost
James Bay Hydroelectric (Quebec)	16.0
Churchill Falls Hydroelectric (Labrador)	1.0
Thames Barrage (U.K.)	1.4
Jubail and Yanbu (Saudi Arabia)	70.0
Sasol, Phases I and II (South Africa)	6.0
King Khaled City (Saudi Arabia)	1.5
Syncrude (Alberta)	3.0
Saudi Gas Gathering	16.0
TAPS (Alaska)	8.0
North Sea Oil—Brent (U.K.)	4.0
Hong Kong Subway	1.0
CSN Steel Plant (Brazil)	2.5
Acominas Steel Plant (Brazil)	4.0
Montreal Olympics	1.5

environment, which contains those factors that have a direct bearing on the ability of the project to meet its cost and schedule requirements. The project environment includes such factors as staff and labor requirements, the availability of services and materials, training requirements, project financing, communications, transportation logistics, distribution and marketing, and the extent and capabilities of local industry. On the outer ring is the general country environment—the one on which most risk-assessment approaches normally focus. This includes factors that have already been mentioned, such as the general political and economic environment, as well as social and cultural problems that will have a direct bearing on project planning and implementation. By identifying and assessing project risk within this framework and using it in conjunction with several basic project-management tools, such as the work-breakdown structure and the task-responsibility matrix, many of the risks associated with the project on both the project level and the general country level can be identified and assessed, and steps can be taken during the initial stages of a project to provide for their later management. Project-management systems are not only applicable during the actual implementation stages of a project, however, when most people consider their use; they are equally appropriate during the feasibility and definition stages of a project.

During the initial feasibility stages of a project, several risks can be

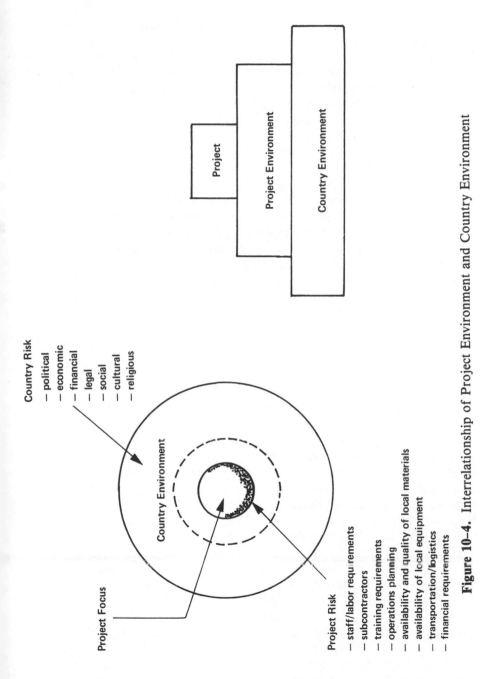

Figure 10–4. Interrelationship of Project Environment and Country Environment

identified and assessed as part of the initial development of the project work-breakdown structure. Are the infrastructure and services available in the host country adequate to assure construction and operation of the project in a timely manner? Some of the specific points that need to be examined are availability and quality of local equipment, supplies, and services; the extent of primary and secondary support industries within the domestic economy; and the level of local professional services and contractors. Will the project require locally produced material? Does it meet the standards required for the project? If so, will local supplies be adequate? What are the projected trends for long-term domestic demand for this product from other sectors of the economy? If there is a large projected increase in demand, will supplies be enough to meet the project's needs during its life?

Once this analysis is performed, it may be decided that there are other alternatives to purchasing from existing local sources. One possibility is to set up local subsidiaries to produce goods locally; another is to import the required materials from abroad. If a decision is made to import goods or services to support the project, has an assessment been made of the local laws and regulations regarding imports of particular materials and the associated time delays and costs?

Another area that should be assessed during the feasibility stage of a project, in connection with the development of a breakdown structure, is the availability of construction equipment. On most large jobs undertaken in the United States, a contractor can either lease or purchase equipment on the basis of favorable supplier credits. By doing so, the contractor reduces initial financing requirements. Often, however, when equipment is shipped overseas, the supplier-credit option is foreclosed. The supplier in this instance may require a letter of credit that provides for payment either when the goods leave the port of origin or upon delivery at the port of the project. Since construction projects in developing countries normally require the importation of a greater proportion of equipment, supplies, and materials than would be needed in a domestic job, the loss of supplier credits of this type and the requirement of letters of credits may increase project costs significantly and reduce cash flows accordingly.

Other risks that must be assessed during the feasibility stages of the project are the availability of skilled and nonskilled labor relative to the employment requirements of the project and the availability of middle-management personnel. Although local labor often is cheaper, additional hidden costs often offset the savings realized from the reduced wages. Foreign labor often is largely unskilled, with a lower level of education and different cultural attitudes toward work than are found elsewhere. This often necessitates the establishment of an extensive on-site training program to teach the skills of modern construction work. Additional costs also result from a higher use of materials and supplies because of waste created by the local work force, which often is unaccustomed to working with the materials and complex machinery on the project.

Even more important than the management and organizational issues associated with many international projects are the financial risks. These should be identified and assessed as early as possible during the feasibility and definition stages of a project, so that the risks associated with the development of the project budget and the cost-control system can be minimized. Some of the financial issues that can have an adverse effect on project budgets and that are often overlooked on many international projects—largely because they have materialized only in the past few years—are the number and types of currency used as payment on the project, floating exchange rates, local currency laws regarding repatriation and convertibility of funds, and, of course, inflation.

Currency differences may present substantial risks to the profitability of a project. On many international projects, the contract currency may not be the same as the local currency or the domestic currency of the contractor. Often, as many as three or more currencies may be involved in the contract. The addition of other foreign subcontractors or suppliers can also increase the number of currencies. Before the advent of floating exchange rates, the use of several currencies on a project did not present much of a problem. Since 1971, however, when floating exchange rates were reintroduced on the world scene, the risk of suffering loss through exchange-rate fluctuations, particularly on long projects, has increased considerably. Alterations in the exchange rate between a number of currencies can rapidly eliminate projected profits or result in large losses if the impacts of this factor are not correctly assessed early in the project.

General economic conditions in a country also can have a sizable impact on the local project environment. With floating exchange rates, high rates of inflation, and the increasing difficulty many less-developed countries have in servicing their external debt, it is not uncommon for currencies to be devaluated during a project. This trend will continue, if not increase in frequency, during the next decade. Another factor that often accompanies a currency devaluation is the implementation of local currency laws that prohibit the repatriation of funds or the convertibility of funds from the currency of the country in which the project is being carried out to other currencies in which the contractor normally operates. Nonconvertibility is usually the result of financial restrictions of the country that is providing the funds to pay for a project's construction, and it is common in many countries that have severe balance-of-payments or debt-servicing problems coupled with a weak economy. Perhaps the most serious economic problem that can indirectly affect the projected returns and cash flow of a project are domestic and international inflation rates. If the duration of a project is greater than eighteen months, the risks that accrue to it as a result of local inflation may be substantial. In some countries, such as Argentina, where inflation is greater than elsewhere, this time frame is obviously smaller. Inflation can affect a project in a number of ways. It can result in a rise in the price of locally available labor and supplies. It may also lead to a monopolization of local goods that are in short supply by the government, which requires them for its own projects. Inflation can also lead to the legislation of large wage increases, which the local government views as a means of compensation for the loss of domestic purchasing power.

In countries where the threat of inflation is high, what can be done to reduce the potential risks that this imposes on a project? First, inflation rates can be indexed into the price of a contract. Without an indexed contract, however, the contractor must estimate future inflation rates as well as possible and thus assume the full risk of what lies in the future. Depending on the state of the local economy and the rate of domestic inflation, the risks vary accordingly. Contractual clauses that allow for an adjustment in the contract price in the event of locally legislated price increases for labor, supplies, or materials are another means of reducing the risks imposed by inflation. The primary contractor should also attempt to spread the risk by requiring subcontractors and major suppliers to follow more or less the same contractual system that the primary contractor is expected to adhere to by the project owner. All subcontracts should be in the same currency as that of the contract. When possible, the prime contractor should also attempt to identify subcontractors and suppliers that are familiar with the region and have worked there before, so that they are aware of the pitfalls of doing business overseas and are able to anticipate many of the problems that accompany international projects.

The last areas of risk that often are not fully identified and assessed during the intitial stages of a project are inventory requirements and costs. On large overseas projects, it is not uncommon for most of the equipment, materials, supplies and spare parts to be imported. The establishment of an on-site inventory often is used as a means of reducing the inherent risk of delay in the project schedule. An on-site inventory provides for timely delivery of materials from numerous overseas suppliers as well as for on-site inspection and timely corrections if these goods do not meet project standards. Purchasing this inventory, however, as well as constructing the facilities to store it and administer it, can be a large additional cost that must be factored into the project budget during the initial feasibility and definition stages. Inventory costs, however, often are not adequately covered in the planning of international projects. An additional problem is that inventory purchases must be financed rather early in a project's life cycle and consequently reduce the project's cash flow. On large projects, the additional cost of establishing on-site inventory as well as the loss of supplier credits can add as much as 50 percent to 100 percent to the value of various materials used on the project.

These are a few examples of the types of risks that will attend large-scale international projects in the forthcoming decade. Some of them existed during the comparatively stable era before the OPEC embargo but on a more manageable scale; others have arisen since that time. Tools and techniques exist to manage these risks, but their existence must be recognized and everything possible must be done to quantify them in the early stages of project planning if such management is to be successful.

11 Project-Management Control: New Needs of Owner-Management

Albert J. Kelley

The approach by owner-management to major project engineering and implementation is undergoing significant change. It is clear that this change is being brought about by cost overruns and schedule slippages that have resulted in increasing owner dissatisfaction with overall project performance; by a recognition that project-management effectiveness must be improved; and by increasing concern by regulatory agencies, special-interest groups, and the general public about the seemingly runaway costs of projects and their impact on product costs.

In the current uncertain economic environment, exacerbated by inflation, project responsibility has moved sharply upward from contractors to project owners. Few owners, however, have sufficient experience in direct project management to fully manage the new responsibilities associated with a major project.

A primary question involves who bears the risk. With previously lower inflation rates, contractors often could sufficiently predict their costs to offer work on a fixed-price-turnkey basis. Thus, with a fixed price and a completion date, risk for cost overruns was borne substantially by the contractor. For these reasons, owner project control was relatively easy.

In the current economic climate, however, these factors have changed. Contractors no longer dare forecast firmly their actual cost to completion. If pressed to offer fixed-price bids, they generally add safety factors or escalation clauses of such magnitude that the bid often becomes noneconomic or meaningless to the owner. Firm, fixed-price contracting is fast becoming a thing of the past and may no longer be an economically viable approach to project management. Cost-reimbursable contracts or fixed-price contracts with various indexes or escape clauses (which may in the long run be more expensive to the owner than cost-reimbursable contracts) not only are becoming popular but, under many conditions, are the only contracting format under which reasonably competitive bids can be obtained.

At the same time, increased finance charges now have a much greater impact on project costs. At 16 percent interest per annum, for example, a delay in project completion can add significantly to the capital costs of a project and can be a considerable percentage of a cost overrun.

In the past, owners typically have engaged designers and constructor-manufacturers to carry out projects, with the owner defining overall policy and identifying design concepts and basic project guidelines. The owner often had minimum direct participation in the management of the project, relying instead on executive-management interface with the designer-constructors. The owner staff responsible for overseeing project activity usually consisted of a few individuals who usually were technically oriented rather than management-oriented. Historically, this approach has been satisfactory, because the regulatory impact on projects was relatively minor and technical and construction performance was fairly predictable; project completion within schedule and cost budgets was the usual case.

The environment in which major projects, particularly construction projects, have been carried out in the past ten years has become increasingly complex. The more demanding regulatory process and the lack of predictability, from both a technical and a regulatory standpoint, has required greater owner involvement in management of projects. In response to a more demanding environment and to unsatisfactory turnkey performance in the past, many owners, including utility industries, have established a trend toward more active participation in management of construction projects. This newly evolving role usually has taken one of three forms.

The first mode consists of formation of a project-management team to monitor the performance of the designer-constructor. The owner team directly manages the resources employed to design and construct the plant. This approach usually requires a modest-sized owner project-management team, with both management and technical skills.

The second mode has been to integrate the owner's project management with designer-contractor management groups. Under this arrangement, often using a salt-and-pepper organization, owner-managers play an active role in the day-to-day supervision of engineering or construction work. A fairly sophisticated level of managerial and technical skills is needed by the owner's project-management team. The size of the owner project management team varies widely, depending on the degree of integration and project characteristics; it is often two to three times larger than the team in the first mode.

In the third mode, a few owners have established in-house groups to perform the work normally performed by the designers or constructors. These owners typically have major ongoing projects. Thus, this approach is found most often in large utilities. A very large total work force is required, and a full range of both managerial and technical skills is needed.

The trend throughout the owner community is toward a more active role for companies in the management of projects. In most cases, a company will still select design or construction firms to accomplish design engineering, to procure materials, and to perform construction. The owner's project-management group usually will focus on implementing overall project policies, guidelines, and design concepts; maintaining visibility over project status; and initiating corrective action as appropriate.

In any of these modes, owners are particularly concerned with monitoring progress because of the need to keep management informed, to report requirements to regulatory agencies, and to manage cash flow. As a result of this growth in owner participation, an increasing need has developed for objective review of project progress.

Since owners have assumed more responsibilities, they require greater control. Owners must obtain project data in order to control overall risk, plan financing needs, plan project strategy, manage contracts, and plan plant start-up and production efforts. Increased owner responsibility and the concomitant capability mean greater owner involvement in the five phases of project implementation: strategy, organization, systems implementation, testing, and start-up and operation.

In federal government projects, the owner, in this case the government, always designates its own project manager and staff, which may be augmented by direct contractor support. The government project manager cannot legally delegate certain responsibilities that belong to the government. The government project manager and his staff establish a precedent for management of projects, which is now being emulated in the private-owner sector and in developing countries.

In developing countries, project management and control are increasingly being exercised by the host country, which often presents paradoxes, since many of these countries do not actually have the capabilities to exercise the owner-management modes defined earlier. In such cases, project-management-support contractors are being employed to provide assistance.

Management-Information Systems

A major project undertaken by a corporate or public entity represents a nexus between the steady-state management of an institutional organization and the transient, ad hoc management approach required for projects. As shown in figure 11-1, the stability and volatility of most major projects is very high, particularly when compared with permanent organizations. A key to effectively bridging these two very different modes of management operation is a substantive and appropriate project-management-information system (MIS). In the past, the project MIS has been established and used primarily to provide information within the project to the project manager and perhaps to his direct superiors. Increased owner involvement, even financial-community involvement, now requires a more sophisticated

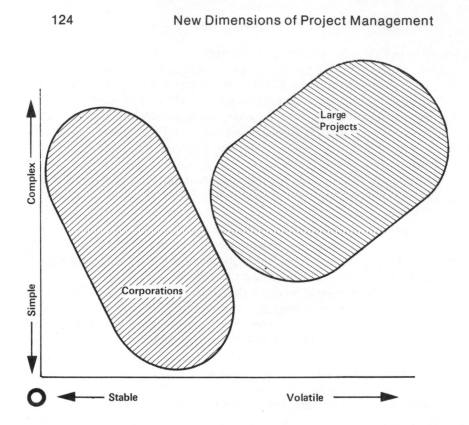

Figure 11-1. Complexity-Volatility Diagram for Corporations and Projects

project MIS that can provide, from the same base data, management information in a form compatible with and useful to the owners and the financiers.

In setting up a project and its MIS, it is important that the needs and requirements of the owner are fully recognized, not only to monitor continually progress of the design, procurement, construction, and start-up, but to project such information in a style that is easily understood by all levels of owner personnel.

Conventional MISs have evolved over a period of years to serve functionally structured permanent organizations. Project MISs have emerged more recently to serve temporary, relatively short-lived multifunctional projects. Compared to the various organizational MISs, project MISs must handle more diverse information and be more predictive and integrated over the time span of use.

A better understanding of the differences and the interfaces between project and organizational MISs can help to resolve current problems and avoid future difficulties in the implementation of information systems that serve operating project managers and owners.

The basic classes of primary MISs may be identified as general management, financial, logistics, business acquisition, and resources, to which we now add projects.

Project MISs enable us to plan, schedule, execute, and control projects—those complex, unique efforts that cut across organizational and functional lines and must achieve specialized results at a particular time and within a given budget. Projects may be viewed as temporary profit centers that subcontract most if not all of the actual work required to complete them. Project managers and the higher-level multiproject managers to whom they report must have MISs that will enable them (1) to plan, subdivide, estimate, integrate, forecast, evaluate, and control all projects, integrating all their life-cycle phases; (2) to integrate action plans, schedules, resources, all identified work breakdown structure (WBS) elements, and organization responsibilities, including estimates, budgets, actual expenditures, physical progress, and forecasts of time and cost to complete; and (3) to allocate resources over multiple projects or schedule activities to use available resources most productively. The key differences between project and organizational MISs are summarized in table 11-1.

Product and Project Planning and Control

In organizing project information, as well as reporting to the owner, a useful breakdown is to separate information into product and project information. Product information or information about the product resulting from the project is of interest to several levels of owner-management. Project-management information involving the execution of the project is primarily of interest to the project team but can be reported to higher levels as necessary and appropriate. Product information can be worked into the overall organizational MIS, while project management information can be kept in a separate project MIS.

The product planning and control functions are (1) establishing and controlling the product characteristics; (2) controlling product configuration; and (3) establishing and controlling product quality. These concern what the end results of the project will be, encompassing information about the physical performance and economic characteristics of the product. Specific tools to carry out those functions, such as plans, procedures, reports, analyses, and reports, relate to the specific product, environment, and industry.

The project planning and control functions are (1) establishing and controlling project plans and objectives; (2) defining the project; (3) planning

Table 11-1
Key Differences between Project and Organizational MISs

	Organizational MIS	Project MIS
Purpose	To manage permanent, slowly changing organizations	To manage temporary, rapidly changing projects
Type of information handled	Each separate MIS deals with specific information of primary interest to one part of the functional organization	Many types of information affecting several functional areas contributing to each project
Time horizon	Usually limited to budget cycle	Reflects the duration of each total project and each life-cycle phase therein; therefore, must be flexible; usually extends beyond the annual budget cycle
Predictive capacity	Limited to budget period; maximum usually one year	Must have strong predictive capacity reaching to the end of each project, usually beyond one year
Integrative capacity	Limited, since each MIS deals with one specific type of information— with the exception of general MISs, which must have integrative capacity the same or even greater than project MISs	High, since information dealing with action plans, time, cost, resources, logistics, and business acquisition must be interrelated and summarized for each project and each affected functional organization.
Ease of implementation	High, if a modular approach is used, since new procedures can be introduced for a limited segment within a function, and since the integrative capacity requirement is limited	Low, since system effectiveness is directly related to the degree of integration, and since project MISs depend heavily on many organizational MISs that frequently have inherent inconsistencies in procedure and data (different numbering schemes, cut-off dates, cycle times, and so forth)

the work (tasks); (4) scheduling the work; (5) estimating required resources (manpower, money, material, facilities); (6) budgeting resources; (7) assigning and authorizing work (internal and external); (8) evaluating progress (physical, cost, manpower, schedule and cost control); and (9) performing integrated evaluation of time, cost, and technical performance. These concern how the end results for the project will be achieved, encompassing information about project objectives, definitions, action plans, resource plans, budget forecasts and expenditures, progress to date, and similar nontechnical matters.

Owner Information

The owner, and particularly his project-management team, should receive project-status data at whatever levels he desires, so that he can monitor and control his project risk. These data should be in the form he needs. The project-status data report to owners must fulfill certain basic requirements, particularly at the higher levels:

1. It should be simple to read.
2. It should not be overdetailed.
3. It should emphasize cost-to-complete and trend data.
4. It should identify possible new funding requirements at the earliest opportunity.
5. It should provide a review of current project problems, with an assessment of their possible impact on project performance (including operational, objectives, cost, and schedule).
6. It should be accurate and reliable.

Few available project-monitoring systems meet these requirements, principally because they are too detailed for owner needs above the direct owner-project team. Furthermore, most project-monitoring schemes tend to be hardware-oriented and give little consideration to factors external to the project, such as the environment, regulations, legal issues, and public interactions. An increasing need in the future will be assistance to the owner and his financial backer in providing a project overview and assessment on a continuing basis, with data that are tailored to the owner's needs. In addition to providing data, the report system to the owner should include sufficient information, so that the owner and his financial backers can assess and analyze project risk to whatever level they may desire.

We have developed various graphic approaches to provide owner-managers the information to meet their needs. In all these approaches, the key is not the format itself but the requirements of the organization, the quality of information developed within the format, its meaning to the organization, and its reporting frequency. One example is project data sheets (figure 11-2), which compress quantitative and qualitative status and trend information into two pages. A more detailed assessment of historical and future trends can be obtained from a program manager's assessment chart (figure 11-3).

For forward planning at several management levels, a flow diagram of key events and decisions can be employed to tie these levels together by integrating ongoing program activities with management review and decision points (figure 11-4).

PROJECT: PROJECT MANAGER
                                             LOCATION

PROGRAM: PROGRAM MGR.
                                             DIVISION

TOTAL EST. COST   Start
CURRENT FY'   Complete

PERFORMING ORGANIZATIONS

   Name   Location of Work   Activity

PROJECT OBJECTIVES:

MARKET FEATURES:

BUSINESS STRATEGY:

PROJECT MANAGEMENT APPROACH:

TECHNICAL APPROACH:

SCHEDULE   **ALL YEAR BASELINE**

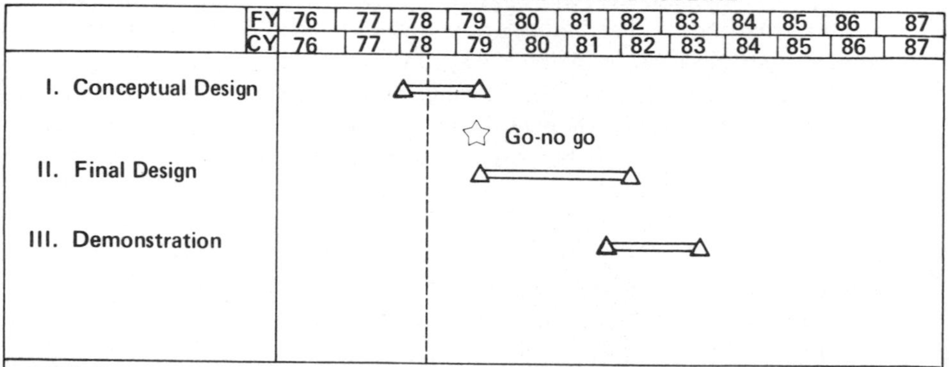

	FY	76	77	78	79	80	81	82	83	84	85	86	87
	CY	76	77	78	79	80	81	82	83	84	85	86	87
I. Conceptual Design													
II. Final Design													
III. Demonstration													

Go-no go

NOTES:

SIGNIFICANT ISSUES AND ACTIONS:

Figure 11–2. Project Data Sheet

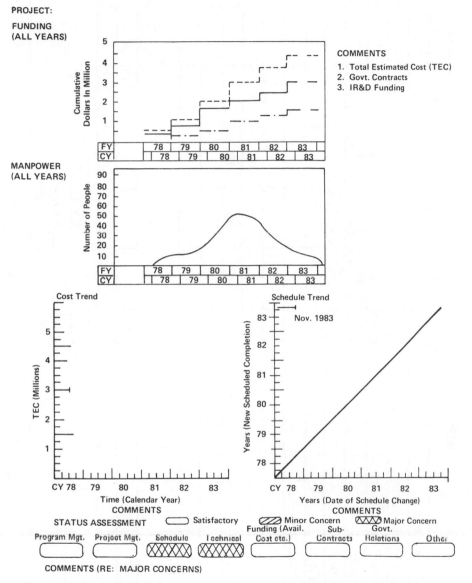

Figure 11-2 continued

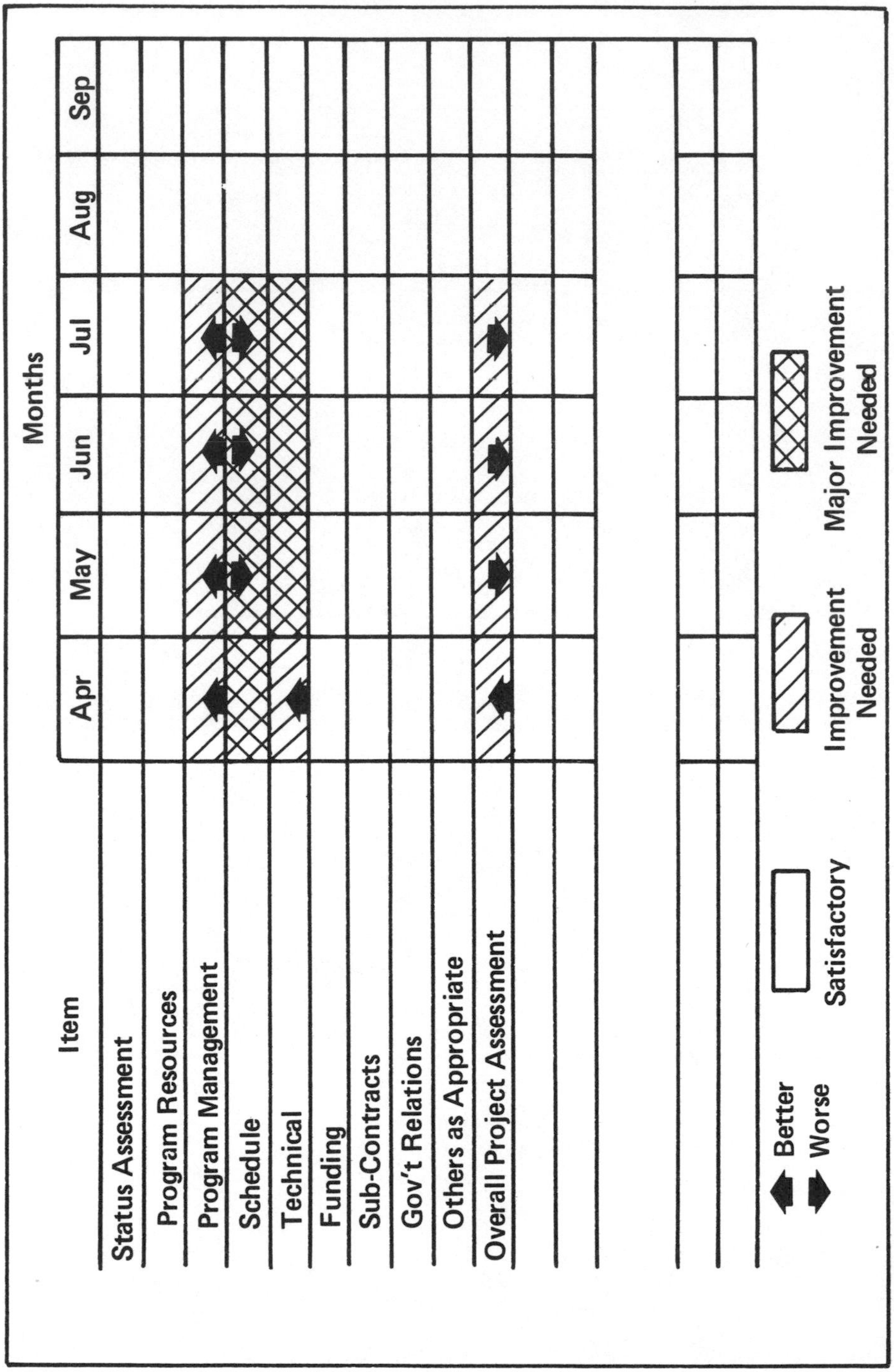

Figure 11–3. Program Manager's Assessment Chart

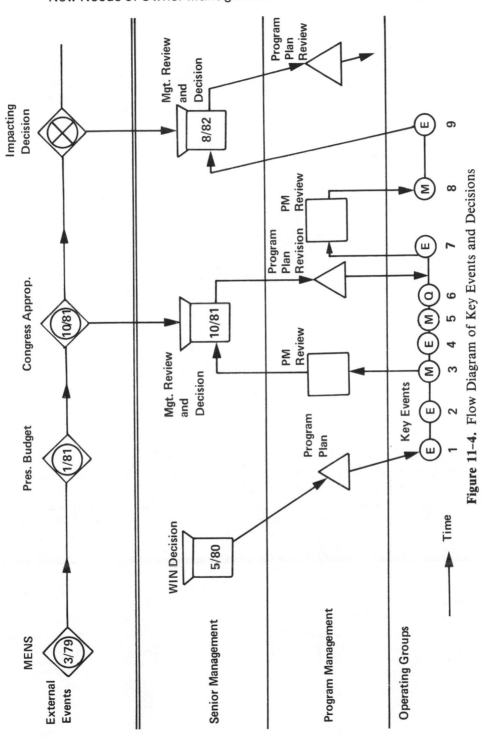

Figure 11-4. Flow Diagram of Key Events and Decisions

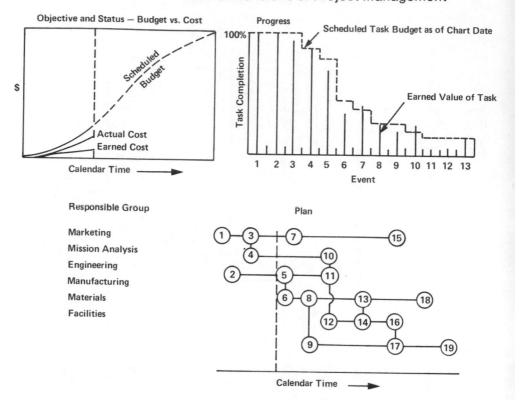

Figure 11-5. Line-of-Balance Progress

For more specific review at the manager level, we have developed a graphic progress report combining elements of PERT, earned-value, and line-of-balance techniques (figure 11-5).

Monthly and quarterly management-review formats have been created to organize project information into categories of interest to both owner-managers and senior project officials. These include current product and market information as well as comprehensive project-status and trend data.

Graphic project reports can be used in making commitments up and down the organization, to provide agreements and understanding equivalent to contracts among project and supporting functional personnel and between project managers and corporate management. Graphics also can be used in making decisions and in communicating them. Finally, graphics can help reduce the number of meetings necessary for project and product coordination.

Conclusion

The project manager now must satisfy many clients with many different types of information. All reports, must stem from the same data base, of course, but many of the higher-level owner and financial-community reports that the project manager will be required to make will contain information and judgments that cannot be put into the data base and that cannot be put into a computer or printed out of a computer. Such information, often qualitative and judgmental, can be just as important at higher levels in the owner organization, the financial community, and regulatory agencies as any data-laden hard-copy printout.

Open communication, both formal and informal, will increase credibility among all segments of the project and owner teams. The selection of the project manager and his management style is as important in accomplishing this end as the appointment of capable staff. The modern project manager's task is multifaceted and is as complex as the project itself. He must be forward-thinking, anticipating not only the direct needs of his project but those of his client and financial backers.

12 Information Technology for Project-Management Control

Ivars Avots

The increasing size and complexity of today's projects requires sophisticated information systems for successful execution. Much of this would not be possible without the great improvements in data-processing technology of the past fifteen years. Cost and schedule correlation, for example, which failed in the early 1960s, can now be achieved readily. Purchasing, inventory, and accounting functions can be integrated with the project-management system. Schedules can be updated almost instantaneously, and three-week delays in receiving monthly cost information are a thing of the past. Complex network relationships can be presented to management as computer-produced multicolor bar charts.

To be able to use these advanced technologies, however, requires hardware of the latest generation. Providing this is not easy when the projects are located in remote parts of the world, where the traditional lines of communication do not reach. In such cases, the types of technology that must be considered include dedicated telephone lines, microwave links, locally established computing centers, and on-site minicomputers.

Dedicated telephone lines represent the least change from traditional information systems, but their cost can be very high, and in some parts of the world their reliability can be very low. Microwave links help to overcome this problem, but they are also expensive; furthermore, in some countries, such as Saudi Arabia, they may be illegal.

Local computing centers have been set up in distant countries by some companies whose volume of project work is large enough to warrant it. This can be cost-effective if the volume of work does not fluctuate greatly or if local associates can be brought in to supplement the venture. Some companies believe, however, that project information is so sensitive that they want to maintain complete physical control over data processing. In this case, an on-site minicomputer may be the best alternative.

Closely tied with the choice among the data-processing alternatives is the decision of what functions will be included in the project information system. As the capabilities of computer systems have increased, management has placed greater demands on them and has extended the scope of project interest from cost and schedule to other functions that affect the

successful completion of a project. Typically, a project information system
may also include equipment management, inventory control, and purchasing and expediting. In offshore projects that have special accounting
requirements, or when the home-office services are not readily available,
the system may also include payroll, accounts receivable, accounts payable,
general ledger, and property accounting. An example of such a system is
shown in figure 12–1.

The most significant difference between recent project information
systems and their predecessors is their interactive capability. Managers are
no longer dependent on a data-processing department to provide turnaround reports but may tap the system at any time through a visual-display
terminal. In addition, special data-processing training is not necessary to
carry on a conversation with the computer.

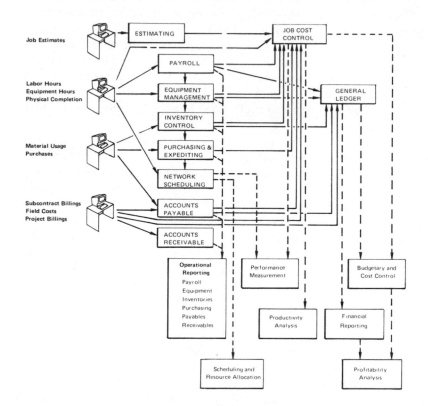

Source: Printed with permission from Construction Information Systems, Inc.

Figure 12–1. Typical Integrated Construction-Project Management System

Although interactive features have been available to corporate planners and financial modelers for some time, their application to project management came only a few years ago, when new minicomputer-based systems were introduced. At present, there are still many mainframe systems that handle project information in a batch mode. The momentum inherent in these large systems and the cost of changing them have provided a shelter for small vendors of systems that are conceptually far advanced. Formerly constrained by the computing capabilities of the minicomputers, these vendors are benefiting from the recent explosion in the capacity of the small machines. It is not unusual to find minicomputer-based systems that match or exceed most of the traditional software offerings.

Given this state of the art, managers find themselves at a crossroads, having to decide whether to lose competitive posture by staying with an old system or risk unknown problems by moving to a new system. Their situation is further complicated by the considerations of central versus distributed processing and the continuing developments in telecommunications networks. Furthermore, it must be recognized that, although there are many bright middle managers who are willing to take the risks associated with a new technology, they often meet resistance at the top management levels, where bad experiences with early computer applications may still be remembered. This undoubtedly leads to such popular responses as: "Use any system you want as long as it can run on our central processor." "We have large projects, we need large computers to handle our data." "We are too busy to play with a terminal." "We make money. There is no need to change our system for the sake of change."

The five best-known traditional project-scheduling and cost-control systems are Project/2 with PCP, MSCS with COPES, PREMIS with PICOM, PMS-IV, and PROJACS. These systems are still favored by companies that require processing of networks containing great detail and extensive processing choices. Typical of such users are public utilities and main offices of large engineering and construction firms. Although a few of them have switched to minicomputer systems, this change has not always been successful. In at least one case, the two systems are used side by side—the minicomputer serving individual projects and the mainframe system integrating the details of many thousands of activities.

Although the principal reason mainframe users are intrigued by minicomputers may be cost, they have also recognized the need for data-base management systems and interactive capabilities that are not provided by all the large project-management systems. Similarly, these users often seek the greater flexibility in reports and the faster reaction capability obtained through the interactive systems.

An issue that may be confusing to a managers who does not have extensive knowledge of computer technology is the difference between mainframe, minicomputers, and microcomputers. The borders between these categories have been rapidly changing as the capabilities of today's mini-computers far exceed those of the mainframe computers of a few years ago. Similarly, the size of the machine is no longer significant; the latest Intel three-chip micromainframe equals the power of today's biggest minicom-puters. One measure of comparison may be cost; mainframe prices are typically seven-digit numbers, minicomputer prices five or six, and microcomputer prices three or four. Another difference may be in the amount of support provided by the manufacturers and vendors. Mainframe computers have been around for many years and have well-established maintenance-support channels, whereas many of the new developments are by vendors who are new in the market and have limited support capabilities.

Frustrations may arise from the fact that many of the new systems are continually growing and increasing in capability. This is because many of the vendors are small and inadequately capitalized, and income from new orders often is used to finance development of the system. It is not unusual to find several package releases during a month, each offering some im-provement over the previous one. These changes can create problems in the comparative evaluation of project-control packages. It is very possible that, given a set of criteria, one may find a package in first place one month and a runner-up the next. Such situations should decrease with the increasing maturity of the systems and with greater competition, which will eliminate some of the poorly managed companies and facilitate consolidations into a few strong ones. This would also reduce the risk that a vendor whose package is selected is no longer in business a year later.

Other items that must be watched when considering systems include salesmen who may promise delivery dates that cannot be met and system features that can be achieved only with considerable manipulation. One of the most serious problems with systems of small vendors is inadequate documentation. If the system is to be deployed offshore, there may also be problems in supporting it internationally. In such situations, special atten-tion should be given to the reliability record of the system. It is worthwhile for the potential user to talk to as many other users as possible to determine their experiences with a particular vendor.

In evaluating small systems, management also requires considerably more technical support than is necessary with the traditional programs. Because of lower hardware costs, and continuous improvements in the capabilities of the small machines, one does not expect to stay very long with the same equipment. There may be a considerably larger investment in the software and associated support systems, however, which one might be reluctant to replace. Therefore, it is important to know whether the pro-posed system will run on later minicomputer models. It is significant that the operating systems used by different manufacturers and even different models of the same manufacturer may be different. This means that the programs may not be readily transferable from one machine to another.

Another problem is that programs often are designed for a particular data-base management system or computer language. It may be very expensive or impractical to convert such programs to run on another machine. There is also a growing tendency among vendors to manipulate the computer's microcode—the functions that are executed through features in the hardware rather than the software part of the system. Such programs are difficult to transport to another machine; if it is done, the programs may lose some of their efficiency.

Other technical considerations that the manager needs to cover include the expected capacity requirements and the possibility of going to a network environment, in which several small computers are connected. Although technically feasible, such an approach may slow down the response capability of the program to the point that it becomes frustrating for the user. Finally, one must look ahead to other potential applications to be used on the same machine. Although such applications may be available to the machine, they may require a different operating system or data base, particularly for project-management versus engineering programs.

Currently popular interactive systems include ARTEMIS (HP-1000), CONSTRUCT (HP-3000, PRIME, MICRODATA), CUE (PRIME), HP-3000), TRACK 50 (PRIME), and VISION (PRIME). Designed specifically for minicomputers, some of these systems are priced as low as $150,000, including the hardware. Although all the systems include network-scheduling and job-cost-control capabilities, there is a considerable difference in the other applications that are available. There is a clear trend among vendors, however, to add the other applications to their basic package and to have them all perform on an integrated basis.

Finally, the manager is faced with frequent announcements of new technological breakthroughs that will further increase the capacities and cost effectiveness of computing. During February of 1981, for example, Intel introduced the so-called micromainframes, priced at around $1,500, which incorporate a large computer capability into three small chips. Companies that have several large projects and could use a dozen or more standalone project-management systems, naturally wonder whether to spend $100,000 for a system now or to wait for a system that may be available at a fraction of the cost. Several points enter into this picture.

First, it usually takes three to four years before new technological developments reach the commercial stage. Although there are several new products that might have a great impact on project-management systems in a few years, management needs the tools to control their projects in the meantime.

Second, the low cost of new processors is no longer as attractive when one considers that it represents only about 5 percent of the cost of a system. Furthermore, while the hardware cost has been going down, the software cost has been increasing, reflecting higher labor costs. Computer peripherals, such as printers, and terminals, have been going down in cost only moderately and will probably reach a bottom level. As a result, the micromainframe may sell for $1,500, but, by the time all the peripheral equipment and operating software are added, the computer may cost as much as $50,000.

Third, the current approach to microcomputer systems has been to increase the throughput of the hardware at the cost of software inefficiencies. This is because software development has not been able to keep pace with hardware developments. As a result, doubling the speed of hardware does not result in doubling the speed of the program.

Finally, the point about maintainability and reliability should be stressed again. A system with the latest technological components will not be of any use to a project in the Middle East if it breaks down and there is nobody to service it. The human links to the system will remain important and often will determine the choice between the latest technology and a well-proven system.

13 Reducing Neglected Risks on Giant Projects

Allen Sykes

Introduction

The Two Main Types of Projects

The special problems associated with managing and accomplishing the very largest projects, those costing many billions of dollars, are of two broad types: (1) public-sector projects, such as the space program, defense projects, education projects, and research programs, in which the ultimate test of worth is not economic but political, military, or social judgments; and (2) projects that must be justified on essentially economic grounds. The latter category embraces all private-sector projects, many government projects, and many projects that are partnerships between companies and government.

The Record on Giant Business Projects

Projects in this category, which I shall call *business projects,* are easier to judge from the viewpoint of whether or not they are worthwhile. Furthermore, it is easier to decide when to abandon them, because a rigorous profit test is the prime consideration. Even so, the record of success of giant business projects is uneven throughout the Western world. Many of the largest business projects have been saved from disaster only by fortuitous circumstances; for example, few of the offshore oil fields in the North Sea being developed in the early 1970s could have survived without the enormous oil-price rises imposed by OPEC. Large quantities of resources are lost yearly in investigating giant business projects that have little or no chance of coming to fruition. Very frequently, those that are constructed have cost overruns, and by unprecedented amounts and percentage rises. Furthermore, there is no widespread confidence that the giant business projects we are now engaged in will necessarily be handled much better than those of the 1970s, because giant-project management is still more art than science.

141

The Distinguishing Features of Business Projects

To try to transfer some of the significant difficulties frequently experienced in giant business projects from the field of art to that of science, I must comment briefly on some of the more important distinguishing features of such projects. First, to qualify as a giant project, an investment must be essentially indivisible—that is, without significant value until it is accomplished in its entirety (for example, an offshore or wilderness oil or gas pipeline).

Second, because of their size, complexity, and risks, all giant business projects are joint ventures of a number of companies and either one or more governments or, occasionally, a large government alone. Nearly always, however, there will be a much larger number of participants (or quasi-participants—those whose consent or cooperation is necessary for a project's success) than there is for normal-sized projects. Furthermore, these participants nearly always will participate directly in project management, in contrast, for example, to the development of even very large oil or gas fields where one of the oil companies involved takes on the main burden of management, as the operator. This means that decision making will be much more prolonged, but both management requirements and the sums involved per participant will be so large that delegation to a single company is unacceptable.

Third, secondment of participants to giant projects is usually unpopular. Because of this, and for other reasons I shall discuss later, few and occasionally none of the senior managers of giant business projects will have had sufficient experience with comparable projects.

Fourth, the risks associated with giant business projects are inescapably large and so cannot be averaged or at least cannot be averaged very easily, because, by definition, even the largest companies in the world cannot be involved in more than very few such projects. Frequently, participants are involved in only one. Hence, because the consequences of failure will be so serious to participants, a high standard of care in identifying and reducing risks is mandatory.

Fifth, no giant business project is likely to be successfully accomplished unless the participants are sufficiently strong financially to see the project through to completion or to be able to accept the full consequences of either abandonment or postponement, no matter when they occur. Projects that cannot pass this fundamental test at all times are either uneconomical or have the wrong participants, or both.

Finally—because of their size, complexity, and risk; because of the number of participants, including the involvement of one or more governments, even if only in giving necessary permissions; because of the disturbance of giant projects in the markets they use and serve; and because of political and environmental pressures—giant business projects take far longer to accomplish than normal-sized projects. Five to ten years is a typical span from serious feasibility study to the end of construction, a daunting period of involvement, particularly for senior management.

Against this background of some of the main distinguishing features of giant business projects, I will discuss certain important but neglected risks and what can sensibly be done about them. Some of my observations will seem rather simple and obvious, but I must emphasize that even the simple and obvious are frequently neglected in the development of giant projects.

Ensuring Compatible Participants

Minimum Numbers

The greater the number of participants involved in a project, the greater the difficulty of accomplishing it. By *participant,* I do not mean only direct participants—that is, owners—but also indirect participants—that is, all those whose consent, cooperation, and enthusiasm are required to see the project through to a successful conclusion. Usually, one can do little about the number and influence of indirect participants, but it is always worth trying. Concerning direct participants, if a problem is recognized, particularly in the early stages of a project, it will often be possible to keep the participants to a minimum. Usually, every direct participant has a relationship with each of the others, as well as complicated relationships with many of the indirect participants—notably, any governments or government agencies involved. Every participant thus adds to the number of interfaces, and every interface is an added contribution to delay, to disharmony, and, if there are too many of them, to disintegration. The first rule, therefore, is to keep the direct participants to an absolute minimum. Five is enough to cope with; more than ten is very difficult; and much more than ten often will be impossible.

Maximum Compatibility

The second rule of participation is to seek maximum compatibility between the participants. If every firm that has some interest in sharing in a project is allowed in, not only will it cause all the difficulties of extra numbers, but it will also needlessly introduce clashes. Smaller companies are less able to bear risks, less able to provide funds, and less interested in many additional benefits that larger companies consider important. The point seems obvious enough, but often little or no effort is made in the early stages of a project to minimize these complications. When, inescapably, too many small or dissident participants are involved, it is worthwhile to incorporate in the joint-venture agreement provisions for majority control or for buying out smaller participants in stated circumstances.

Overall Project Organization

Allowing for Fluctuating Participation

It is becoming widely recognized that giant business projects pose many new organizational problems, which must be adequately solved if such projects are to be accomplished. The experience of more typical joint-venture partnerships of perhaps two or three companies, in more normal-sized projects, will often be an imperfect guide to the optimum organization of giant projects. Given that a giant business project typically will take five to ten years to completion of construction, it should be apparent that the interest of initial participants may wax or wane, and that some of the eventual key participants may not become involved until some years after commencement. Thus, it will be necessary to provide for the late entry of some participants and for the departure before completion of others. If such happenings are not to ruin a project, a far-seeing and flexible participation agreement will be needed, one that will be drawn up in recognition of the minimum participation that will always be needed to maintain sufficient momentum. This perspective reinforces the previously identified need for ensuring a minimum achievable number of compatible participants.

Frequently, when the exploitation of a giant resource is being actively considered, two or more rival consortia will be formed to develop it. Prior to project award, some companies may well be tempted to switch allegiance, a switch that may mean the success of one group and the demise of another. The longer the period between the resource discovery and the final commitment to construct, the greater the risk of switching. As I shall argue later, this consideration has a profound bearing on the management of a giant-business-project consortium, for it will be obvious that a management drawn entirely from an existing consortium membership may be incapable of winning the project if the membership may change significantly and certainly if it should be made to change in the interest of the project's success.

Decisiveness within the Critical Period

A second problem exacerbated by the long gestation and planning period of giant business projects is that the opportunity for developing a particular resource is seldom without a critical time limit. Because the impact on a market of the output from a giant project is inescapably very large, customers cannot be indifferent to if and when the project will be realized.

Hence, one of the most critical tasks in the early stages of a giant project is to identify the acceptable period in which a decision on the project must be taken or the opportunity either postponed for many years or perhaps lost forever. A critical early task for the project's senior management, then, is to assess whether it is really feasible to reach an acceptable decision to proceed within this time limit. Too rosy a view of this prospect is a frequent cause of unnecessarily wasted effort, but it takes great experience to estimate this matter realistically.

It should be apparent that I am discussing an *economic* opportunity. A belief often grows among the participants, particularly the senior management, of nearly every giant business project that, somehow, its accomplishment is inevitable. Nothing could be further from the truth. The failure rate of giant business projects to get off the ground is unbelievably high, and only the most skilled and determined effort within the critical period will accomplish them at all.

From this discussion, it will be apparent that a highly competent and relevant organization will be necessary. This organization must come to terms with the fact that participants will almost never agree to delegate to the project management sufficient authority for spending very large sums. Every stage of the project must be considered separately and approval given for the next stage. At no stage is this more true than for the completion of construction. It is a common observation that very large projects almost inevitably suffer from huge capital overruns. This means that all giant projects will pass through several major crisis. The best that can be hoped for in any project organization is that the major decisions will be made on a majority basis, because absolute unanimity usually will prove impossible. When the dissenting minority are unhappy, they must be prepared either to go on with the project, to reduce their interest, or, ultimately, to be bought out. Given that the dissenting minority usually will have committed large sums by these decision points, there should be a carefully negotiated procedure for buying them out, for allowing them a carried interest, or for providing some equivalent acceptable outcome. Even with a majority voting system, however, each direct participant will need to call its own major board meetings to consider approving every large expenditure. Although this inevitably prolongs decision making, it is unrealistic to expect otherwise. This consideration reinforces the point already made—that all participants should be strong enough for whatever calls may be made on them.

The Need for a Continuous, Comprehensive Project Overview

Given all the very special features of giant business projects, it is necessary to know that every critical aspect of the project will be under continuous study and review. Without this, a desirable project is in danger of failing because the requirements of some key participant, either direct or, more usually, indirect, have not been met. It is rare, of course, for the major aspects of projects not to be properly studied. Technical, construction, logistical, marketing, and financial problems usually are investigated thoroughly, but political, environmental, legal, tax, insurance, and other aspects frequently fail to receive sufficient consideration. Just as important as these matters are those referred to already—the need to ensure that sufficient key participants, direct and indirect, will remain committed to the project within the acceptable critical period. Given the changing interests of many of these participants over the long periods involved, it is vital that the project be studied continuously from the viewpoint of each of these participants. If it then emerges that the interest of a participant is weakening, it is possible for the project's senior management to set about either rekindling their interests, settling their difficulty, or eventually replacing them with another acceptable participant. The aim is the same as that for all wisely conducted enterprises—to make sure that there are no avoidable major surprises.

This desirable state of affairs is only possible if the senior managers of the project make it their business to have a continuous, comprehensive project overview that covers all these matters. This must be done from the feasibility study until the conclusion of the project, or until its postponement or abandonment. This requirement may seem obvious, but, in my experience, it is rarely done and certainly rarely done comprehensively to the necessary standard. As I have mentioned, it is not common for most of the senior management on a giant business project to have had sufficient experience with other such projects. They are therefore engaged in the understandable but wasteful business of learning what others already know well.

Providing the Appropriate Senior Management

Project Unpopularity

Giant business projects are usually unpopular with managers in participating companies, particularly the most ambitious managers. Why is this so? First, such projects go on for so much longer than normal large, company-based projects; their length and outcome are unpredictable; and they are subject to seemingly endless delays, such that those involved frequently cannot use their best skills fully. Furthermore, the difficulties causing these frustrating delays are often mainly or entirely outside the control of the senior managers involved. The major delays and difficulties imposed by political, environmental, and native-rights pressure groups are often new to most of those involved, certainly in their intensity. Such pressures and delays are never enjoyable. It is therefore not surprising that those who work on giant business projects often work on only one and then say "Never again." Indeed, it is difficult to work in a senior capacity on more than two giant business projects in the course of a career if the projects last the usual five to ten years, even if few people are needed for more than a few years. Thus, the relevant experience for the senior posts is not easily gained, and many giant projects must do without it. Furthermore, it is rare for the lessons of any giant projects to be properly documented, particularly in the United States, where litigation threats can make such a procedure hazardous. The really glamorous or controversial projects may provoke a spate of books, but unless these books are written by those at the very top, and unless they are written from carefully recorded contemporary notes (memory is a poor guide for a project with a five- to ten-year span), they are often so distorted and incomplete as to be largely valueless. If the hard-won lessons are to be properly learned, however, some effort is required of senior management to keep a continuous, relevant record of events—if only for the use of their own companies. This requires considerable discipline, because, given the long hours and strain of running giant business projects, the last thing most of us want to do is keep proper comprehensive records.

Even when participating companies recognize the special management and staffing problems of giant business projects, however, they nevertheless may find it very difficult to assign enough of their most capable people for a sufficient period. Many of the best men assigned by participants to joint ventures fear that their prospects in their own companies will suffer if they are away too long, particularly if their best and often brilliant achievements are not fully appreciated by their distant headquarters. Because of this understandable fear, there is no certainty of getting the best men from participating companies in the first place, or of keeping the ones that are available for as long as project needs dictate. It is not uncommon, for example, to find that the best engineering talent in a participating company is working on a major internal project, in which the potential profitability and the capital cost are much lower than on the giant project in which the company is participating. It may be much more congenial to work on the internal project, however, and it may be even more important to the company.

The Need for Greater Multidisciplinary Skills

Another major concern is that giant projects often call for rather different skills from those that have been developed in even very large companies. It will be apparent from the much larger number of participants in giant business projects and the far greater number of constraints involved that it is much more necessary to compromise between the different disciplines involved. The most satisfactory engineering solution may cause too much environmental opposition. The optimum size of the project may simply be beyond the available finances. The choice of the best contractors for all jobs may not be possible because of the need to employ as many local or native firms as possible. The same can apply to labor and to suppliers. Thus, inevitably, balance and compromise are more prominent in giant business projects than in smaller ones. This puts the skill of multidisciplinary managers at a premium. If it is desired to have sufficiently experienced, multidisciplinary people for the senior management positions (I consider it mandatory), then internal recruitment among the major participants may be inadequate.

Some Solutions

Although there are many specific problems in successfully accomplishing giant projects, once the problems are recognized, they are capable of solution. I believe that the prime requirement is to have an inner project-directing group that will be responsible for recommending policy to the project board and for implementing policies once agreed. The essence of this inner directing group—the most senior management team—is that their loyalty is owned exclusively to the project, that is, to the collective group of direct participants that comprises the owners. Their loyalty is not to any particular participant; indeed, they may be handicapped if this is even suspected. The correctness of this view will be reinforced when it is remembered that memberships of project consortia often fluctuate. This inner group will be concerned with accomplishing and, of course, optimizing the project, so long as it merits accomplishment; recommending postponement when this is the best course; and, if and when justified, recommending abandonment.

The senior management of a project can accomplish this demanding task only if it is sufficiently experienced in other giant business projects and if it is multidisciplinary. The experience of other giant business projects is always desirable, and it is essential on the really difficult projects. Given the peculiar difficulties encountered on giant projects, it is more important that experience has been gained on other giant business projects—almost regardless of the technology or industry involved—because the distinguishing features of giant projects are functions of size rather than of type of project (provided the experience gained was on business as opposed to nonbusiness giant projects). It is also important that this top-management team be multidisciplinary. Relevant multidisciplinary experience is not often acquired in conventionally organized large projects that are owned and managed by a single firm, even when the project itself is very large, yet time and again the critical decisions on giant projects require a good working knowledge of a great many subjects. In large organizations, it is common to find that the most capable people do not branch out into a multidisciplinary method of working until their middle to late forties—sometimes later. This explains why expenditures in the preconstruction phases of projects tend to concentrate on what the project management know best. Because most such managements are dominated by engineers, the engineering aspects of problems receive the most attention. It is rare for other problems (political, organizational, and often marketing and financing) to receive the attention they deserve from a small, tightly knit, powerful team with the power of rapid decision making.

Given the need for thoroughly experienced, multidisciplinary senior management, the recruitment for many of the top positions is likely to be outside the senior management of the participant companies. Once the point is grasped that experience on other giant business projects is the prime requirement, the field for recruitment is widened considerably. It is not enough, however, to have management of the right caliber and experience. If their loyalty is to be to the project, and if at all times they are to be sufficiently objective to accomplish it in the best way or to recommend its postponement or abandonment, then unique remuneration terms are required. It is clear from giant business projects that are exclusively in the public sector that they can have a life of their own, unrelated to their economic viability. If a special team is recruited to manage a giant business project without a special remuneration package, many of its members will be tempted to continue these projects well beyond the point at which they should be let go. I cannot prescribe a precise, ideal form of remuneration, but it must be one that gives top management the confidence to be entirely objective. Perhaps if the managers are guaranteed three years' remuneration beyond the termination of the project prior to the commitment to construct, or an equally or preferably more attractive bonus if it is accomplished within some agreed terms, then they will have the necessary incentive to identify totally with the interests of the direct participants. Clearly, this problem deserves the most careful attention, because the sums involved are trivial compared to the gain to the direct owners from an entirely objective and competent senior management. The sums expended to the decision point on whether to construct typically are in the range of 1.5 percent to 5 percent of final capital cost. On giant business projects, these expenditures can amount to hundreds of millions of dollars, so only the most objective advice is acceptable. Total integrity is worth almost any price.

The basic remuneration of the senior managers will be high by conventional standards, of course, because they will be required to stay with the project over the extended period necessary to investigate it and either accomplish or abandon it, and they must put up with all the inescapable frustrations and delays.

In addition to having the most competent and objective senior management on a giant business project, it is always worthwhile for the owners to have access to other objective advice. I am particularly attracted by the arrangement I have seen on a few such projects in North America, in which the owners are advised by a distinguished panel of experts. These usually are men in the last phase of their careers, or even recently retired, who are acknowledged international experts in their fields. They usually meet three or four times a year for about a week to review all the main problems of the project, the policy options, and the terms of reference for the senior management, and generally to advise on the major problems of project accomplishment. They, too, mainly have multidisciplinary backgrounds and will be expert in at least one or two major fields. They have worked on successful giant business projects but are now at that stage of their career when they do not wish total involvement. The right panel of experienced experts under a good chairman should be worth its weight in gold. It should also reinforce the independence and confidence of the senior project managers. Such a panel also forms an ideal group to conduct a review of each major stage of the project's life, including the crucial final review at the end of the project completion.

If both of these recommended approaches are followed, the owners can be sure that no major matters are likely to be neglected and that the best knowledge, techniques, and experience are brought to bear on their project.

Government Personnel

Solutions of the type discussed in this chapter are only now beginning to emerge after the experience of the giant projects of the 1960s and 1970s. What is done twice is done better; what is done three times is done better still. Therefore, we should always expect improvement in our understanding of how to accomplish these very large projects. It is the experience of the management of such projects, however, that similar improvement is desirable on the part of involved governments. After some great difficulties that have caused considerable increases in construction costs and schedules, it is apparent that it is dangerous and undesirable to try to increase the standard and detail of government regulation by huge steps. This is being recognized increasingly by the wiser governments, which are rethinking their approach to the regulation of giant business projects. Such a reappraisal is to be welcomed and encouraged, since these projects can be accomplished satisfactorily only if all parties involved are working to sensible terms of reference and are trained for and experienced in their tasks.

Realistic Long-Term Contracts

Discussion of neglected risks on giant business projects also requires a brief word on the need for ensuring realistic long-term contracts. By this I mean contracts, particularly sales contracts but also royalty agreements, and the like, that allow for inflation. Until the early 1970s, inflation in the Western world, particularly in North America, was at such a low annual rate that long-term contracts without escalation provisions or with only minimal provisions were common. The massive worldwide price explosions of the last eight years, however, have conferred a massive transfer of benefit from project owners to their customers, to the point where some projects are earning only miserable returns. If this situation is to be avoided—and it is perhaps the biggest factor in profitability for a number of very large energy-based projects—then the most careful provisions must be negotiated before it can be decided whether a project is worth a commitment. This means that current cost-accounting principles must become widely understood and implemented. The same applies to long-term royalty agreements of the kind wherein there is a deduction from gross royalties for the appropriate share of capital and operating costs. There are a number of current examples of contracts whereby a government or its agency is receiving gross royalty on sales but the selling price is not fixed but is free to rise to world levels; the cost deduction is based on historic cost, however. This can lead to a massive and unforeseen burden on those projects. On a number of giant business projects, neglecting to negotiate realistic long-term contracts that take cognizance of increasing costs is by far the largest single risk to profitability.

Reference

Sykes, Allen. "The Project Overview—The Key to Successful Accomplishment of Giant Projects." Proceedings of the international conference, "A Multidisciplined Study of Problems of and Solutions to Successfully Accomplishing Giant Projects," London, May 1978.

**Part V
Organizing and Managing
Human Resources**

14 Project Organizations: Structures for Managing Change

Peter W.G. Morris

A project is a process for achieving defined change. It has a specific, empirically defined objective. We know when the objective has been achieved, and, at that point, the project's work is accomplished and the project is disbanded. Projects follow a set process in accomplishing their objectives. The process involves (1) planning and implementing work in certain predefinable subsystems; (2) creating an organization that to some extent follows specific project lines; (3) implementing project-control systems that must report certain predefinable data; and (4) following a specific life cycle, which is common to all projects. Projects accomplish change—driving through time to something new and different. Thus, by definition, a project is not an ongoing activity.

Many management situations are defined-change situations—situations as diverse as movie making, aerospace, electioneering, aid administration, management consulting, and turnaround situations (see appendix A).[1] Each such situation can benefit from project techniques, management, and organization.

Organizationally, projects are highly distinctive. They are extremely goal-oriented, temporary, and in constant change, and they follow a life cycle of change segments that involves progressing through markedly different phases of work. Conflict is high, since groups working on the project may be new to each other and may have substantially different objectives and styles of work, roles are often vague, priorities are constantly changing, and objectives invariably conflict.

The Project Life Cycle

All projects move through a life cycle (see figure 14–1). Usually, the life cycle involves four distinct phases. The first phase is a feasibility study, involving agreement on project sizing, finance, schedule, organization and location. In the second phase, planning and design, technical definition of the project is expanded: schedule, budget, and financing are refined and reassessed; contracting strategy is defined; permits are sought; and infrastructure and logistics systems are defined. The third phase is production, in

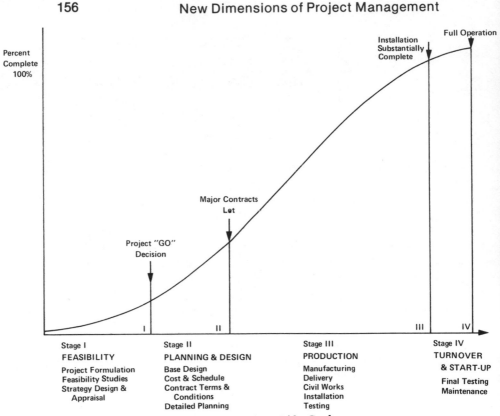

Figure 14-1. Project Life Cycle

which equipment is ordered, manufactured, and delivered; civil work is undertaken; and equipment and facilities are installed. The fourth phase involves turnover and start-up (which overlaps production), in which operations planning is completed, the project is tested and finished, and the operating systems are commissioned. The project life cycle has a number of distinctive features:

1. It is common to all projects.
2. The four phases are dramatically different.
3. The interfaces between the four phases act as important checkpoints in the project's development.
4. The work of the life cycle follows an institutional-strategic-tactical sequence.

Each of the four life-cycle phases is dramatically different from the others in mission, size, technology, and scale and rate of change. These differences create distinctive characteristics of work, personal behavior, and direction and control. Thus, the management style of each of the phases also is dramatically different. Consider, for example, the design and production phases. In the design phase, the objective is to create a design that fulfills the criteria laid down in the feasibility stage. The project organization is relatively small, the work is cerebral and creative, the control emphasis is on estimating rather than on monitoring, and schedule pressure is not tight on a daily-work-level basis. Once the project moves into production, however, most of this changes. The objective then is to make something as efficiently as possible according to the blueprints developed in the design phase. The work often is intensely physical and active. The project increases in size dramatically, moving from perhaps dozens to thousands or even tens of thousands of people. The groups involved are much more tightly organized, on a mechanistic basis, as opposed to design's organic basis.[2] Control involves very tight monitoring to ensure that work is accomplished within the design targets, and schedule pressure is extremely tight.

As design and production are radically different from one another, so are the other phases substantially different. The feasibility stage is small and at a very high level, posing decisions that require considerable judgment. The turnover and start-up phase involves the joint work of people in a variety of subsystems, with a variety of interests and work practices.

The work in each phase has an important, fixed, managerial relationship to that of the other phases. The work of the feasibility stage is highly institutional, involving top management; decisions made in this phase have an overriding impact on the later health of the investing enterprises. The design work is strategic, laying the axes which the tactical work of production will rest. The fourth phase involves a mixture of these three levels of work. Although it would be wrong to suggest that the work during each of the first three stages is exclusively institutional, strategic, or tactical, there is a relative dominance of such concerns during each phase.

Three Key Management Levels

The notion that there are three principal levels of management in an organization—institutional, strategic, and tactical—goes back at least to the work of Talcott Parsons.[3] Parsons showed that each of the levels has an essential role to play in any successfully regulated enterprise: the technical-tactical level (Level III) manufactures the product, middle management (Level II) coordinates the manufacturing effort, and, at the institutional level, top management (Level I) connects the enterprise to the wider social system. Each of the three levels has a fundamental role to play in the management of every project (although distinctions between the levels tend to become blurred on the smaller projects). Surprisingly, however, most project-management literature deals only with Levels II and III. There is little in the literature dealing with such issues as the role of the owner and his financier; relations with the media, with local and federal government, with regulatory agencies, and with lobbyists and community groups; and sizing and timing of the project in relation to product demand and the cost of finance. These are all key issues to project management in the 1980s.

The distinction between Levels II and III is crucial, since it is essentially the distinction between the project and its outside world (see figure 14–2). Levels II and III deal almost exclusively with such familiar project activities as engineering, procurement, installation, testing, and start-up. Level III provides the technical input, and Level II provides both a buffer from the outside world and guidance in avoiding external pitfalls. No project exists in isolation from outside events, however. Level I thus provides coordination of the project with outside events and institutions. Level I actors typically include the project owner and his finance team, government agencies, community groups, very senior project management, and one or two special project executives specifically charged with external affairs, such as public relations and legal counsel.

The involvement of each of these levels is different during each of the major phases of the project life cycle. During the feasibility stage, the owner and his team (Levels I and II) must make crucial decisions about the technical performance and business advantages they are to receive for their investment and, indeed, about whether or not the project should go forward. Once the decision to go ahead is taken, the weight of the work moves to the design team (Levels II and III). During the production phase, engineering reaches a detailed level. Both senior project management (Level II) and technical staff (Level III) are now at full stretch, while the owner (Level I) takes a more reduced monitoring role. Finally, during turnover and start-up, all three levels typically are highly active, as engineering work gets completed (Level III), often under intense management pressure (Level II), while high-level coordination is required at the owner level in coordinating the initiation of start-up activities. The management skills required at each of the levels also are substantially different. At Level III, normative, mechanistic techniques are appropriate, but, at Level I, the emphasis is on judgment and financial and political skills.

Recent investigation of 1,416 projects showed that, on the average, projects overrun up to 60 percent, with those of $1 billion or more overrunning an average 150 percent.[4] The fact that most projects overrun is now becoming widely accepted[5] and is forcing owners and financers to be more stringent in their scrutiny of initial project estimates. This factor and the reluctance of contractors to accept fixed-price contracts when inflation is so high also are making Level I managements more demanding of their professional staff.[6] At the same time, projects have been coming under severe

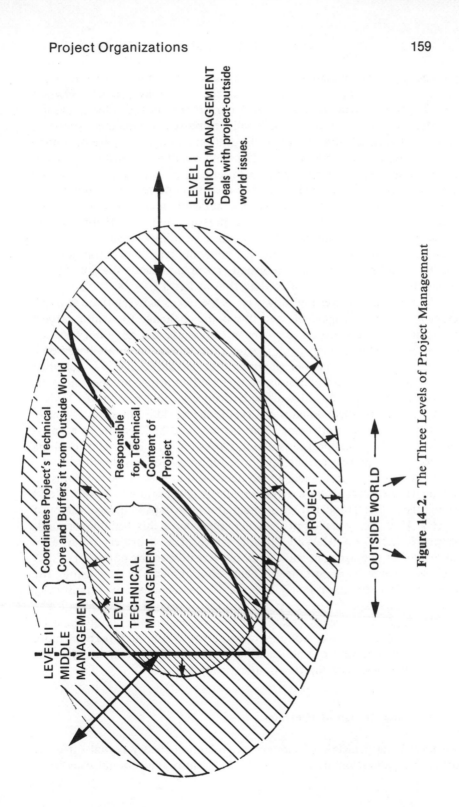

Figure 14-2. The Three Levels of Project Management

pressure from government and citizen groups. Regulatory control is now a major reason for delays and increased costs in many projects. Owners increasingly are having to answer for their projects in the political arena.

Most of the techniques traditionally employed in managing projects, such as network scheduling and configuration management, are of limited value in handling such externalities. The skills required are, instead, those of top business. Such strategies as the maintenance of fall-back positions and security cloaks and such skills as public relations and political lobbying are required. Levels II and III, however, are eminently more suited to management by such systems techniques. The pressure at Levels II and III are typical of those of manufacturing: meeting deadlines, assuring resource availability, and the like. The issues are generally reasonably clear. In contrast to Level I pressures, they are usually more immediate; the time fuse at Levels II and III is much shorter than that at Level I.

What is really interesting, however, is the nexus between these two different modes of management, and this is the challenge for senior project management. Senior project management must use and rely on a systems-analysis perspective of the world, in which rational decisions are based on a trade-off of costs and benefits, planning tools enable managers to schedule and monitor events with precision, and, if conflict arises, an open dialogue between people of goodwill will lead to an amicable resolution. Unfortunately, in the political domain of Level I, the world is not always so nice. Different people have different value systems and hence come to surprisingly different rational decisions about, for example, the merits of projects such as nuclear power stations, airports, highways, or missile silos.

Thus, senior project management needs and uses both the mechanistic, systems view of organization behavior that is appropriate to Levels II and III and the political model of adjustment among groups of diverse values of Level I. How many senior project managers have this training or skill, however? The Trans Alaskan Pipeline survived as a project because its senior project management was incredibly sensitive to the political realities of Congress and the importance of being environmentally responsible; the American SST program failed because its management was politically unsophisticated and failed to get the support it needed in Congress.[7] The Apollo program succeeded because of the political protection given it by NASA, the White House, Administrator James Webb, and, perhaps more important, a tidal wave of public support.[8] How will the many energy programs of the 1980s develop this political support?

Organizational Design of Projects

The underlying principle of modern organization theory is that different forms of organization are required for different organizational situations.

The organizational system—its structural configuration, control systems, culture, and so forth—depends on many diverse factors: the technical features of the work, the amount of managerial and technical coordination required, the quantity and relative importance of different aspects of the work, the specializations involved, the age and size of the enterprises involved, the geographic and market spread, the characters of the individuals and institutions involved, the environment, and so on.[9] This is the so-called contingency theory of organization, which claims (1) that there is no single, right structure for an organization; (2) that organizational change is often inevitable, necessary, and useful; and (3) that subsystem interdependency is especially important to organizational effectiveness.

The contingency theory of organization encourages attention to behavior at the organization's boundaries, points at which interactions take place and change can be most easily monitored. The major part of project management's job is integrating the work of others to achieve the project's technical, cost, and schedule goals. This involves managing performance at the organization's boundaries and interfaces. Several boundaries and interfaces can be identified as typical to all projects. Those at Level I naturally tend to be broader than those at Levels II and III. The principal Level I subsystems are project definition (including technical content, cost, and schedule), operations and maintenance, sales and marketing organization, environment (outside groups), manpower, and commerce and finance. At Levels II and III, the principal subsystems are project definition, organization, environment, and infrastructure. These are what might be called the static or ongoing subsystems, for projects have another vitally important type of subsystem boundaries and interfaces—the life-cycle subsystems, which generate dynamic interfaces.

Dynamic interfaces between life-cycle (or activity) subsystems are of the utmost importance in project management—first, because of the continuous importance of schedule in all projects; second, because early subsystems (such as design) exert a managerially dominant role over subsequent ones (such as manufacturing). Such interrelationships require careful handling if minor mistakes in early systems are not to pass unnoticed and then snowball into larger ones later in the project.

Boundaries should be positioned where there are major discontinuities in technology, territory, time,[10] or organization. Major breakpoints in the project life-cycle—as, for instance, between the four major phases but also between subsystems within each phase (for example, between manufacture, inspection, delivery, warehousing, installation, and testing or between different organizations)—provide important dynamic interfaces. These serve as checkpoints at which management can monitor performance. Most major dynamic interfaces are used in this way. The project feasibility report, the initial project technical design, the formulation and negotiation of the production contracts, and testing and hand-over review points, for example, may also be introduced for purely control purposes without any natural discontinuity, such as design-freeze points, estimates-to-complete, or monthly reports.

Of the three principal types of interfaces that have now been identi-fied—the three levels of management, static subsystems, and dynamic sub-systems—some are clearly larger and more important than others. Organi-zation theorists measure interface size in terms of the degree of differentia-tion between subsystems. Typical measures of differentiation include dif-ferences in organization structure, interpersonal orientations, time horizons, and goals and objectives.[11]

The size of subsystem differentiation is one side of the equation of how much subsystem integration is required. Research has shown that the need for organizational integration increases when (1) the goals and objectives of an enterprise make it necessary to work together closely; (2) the environ-ment is complex or changing rapidly; (3) the technology is uncertain or com-plex; the enterprise is changing rapidly; or (5) the enterprise is organiza-tionally complex. Despite these insights, however, choosing the degree of integration required across an interface inevitably calls for considerable judgment. There is no easy answer to the question of how much manage-ment is enough, but there are some pointers available. In his classic book, James D. Thompson observed that there are three kinds of interdepen-dency, each requiring its own type of integration.[12] The simplest form, pooled interdependence, requires only that people obey certain rules or standards. The next simplest form, sequential interdependence, requires that interdependencies be scheduled. Reciprocal interdependence, the most complex kind, requires mutual adjustment between parties. In project terms, subsystems that are in continuous interaction require liaison in order to achieve the necessary integration, whereas those that just follow on from one another can follow plans and schedules (see figure 14–3).

Several devices can be used to achieve liaison: liaison positions, task forces, special teams, coordinators (or permanent integrators), full project management, and matrix organizations.[13] Each of these options provides stronger integration than the one before. The primary function of liaison positions is to facilitate communication between groups. The liaison posi-tion carries no real authority and little responsibility other than this. Task forces are much stronger. They provide mission-oriented integration in that a group is formed specifically to provide integration for a particular task. Upon completion of the task, the task force disbands. Special teams serve a purpose similar to that of task forces, but they attend to regularly reoccur-ring types of problems rather than to specific issues. A coordinator, or per-manent integrator, provides a similar service as that provided by a liaison position but has some formal authority. He exercises this authority over the decision-making processes but not over the decision makers themselves.

1. Pooled Interdependence

- Participants pool resources, etc.,
  e.g., membership of a club

- Coordination by standards, rules

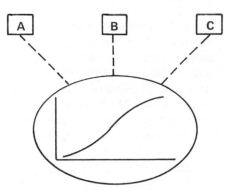

2. Sequential Interdependence

- Participants follow each other
  sequentially

- Coordination by schedule

3. Reciprocal Interdependence

- Participants interact

- Coordination by committee
  or other such liaison device —
  i.e., by mutual adjustment

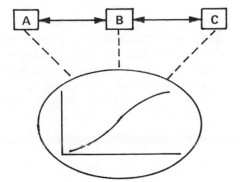

Figure 14-3. The Three Types of Interdependence

This is a subtle but important point, and it often causes difficulties in projects. The coordinator cannot command the persons he is coordinating to take specific actions; that power rests with their functional manager. He can influence their behavior and decisions, however, either through formal means, such as managing the project's budget and schedule or approving scope changes, or through informal means, such as his persuasive and negotiating skills. The role of the full project manager upgrades the authority and responsibility of the integrator to allow maximum cross-functional coordination. The integrator—the project manager—now has authority to order groups directly to take certain actions or decisions.

By general consent, matrix organizations are considered to be the most complex form of organizational structure. Matrix structures provide for maximum information exchange, management coordination, and resource sharing. Matrices achieve this by having staff account simultaneously to the integrating (project) managers and the functional managers whose work is being integrated. Both project managers and functional managers have authority and responsibility over the work, although there is a division of responsibility; the functional manager is responsible for the "what" and "by whom," and the project manager decides the "when" and "for how much." Unfortunately, the person who often suffers most in the matrix is the poor soul at Level III who actually is doing the work. He reports to two bosses—his project manager and his functional manager—which is not necessarily a problem in itself except when, as often happens, the project manager and functional manager are in conflict (for instance, over how much should be spent on the project).

Controversy regarding the relative merits of the matrix organization versus the full-fledged project organization among the hardy perennials of project management. Various writers at various times have offered all kinds of reasons why one form or the other is better. Three points seem to stand out, however. First, the full project-management role—with a project manager in overall command of the project—offers stronger leadership and better unity of command. It is better for achieving the big challenge. Second, the matrix organization is more economical on resources. For this reason alone it often is almost unavoidable on large or complex projects. Third, it is very common to find a full-fledged project manager at the top of a matrix structure. The two forms are not incompatible but in fact fit together rather well—the top project manager (Level I) providing the leadership and ultimate decision-making authority, the matrix providing maximum middle-management (Levels II and III) integration.

Principles of Large-Project Organization

The Trans Alaskan Pipeline (TAPS) remains one of the largest and most ambitious recent superprojects. Constructed at a cost of approximately $8 billion, the project involved installing a 48-inch-diameter insulated pipe carrying hot oil from Prudhoe Bay on the north slope of Alaska over 800 miles of permafrost and mountains—in territory that was substantially unsurveyed—to Valdez, where a huge terminal was constructed that was capable of withstanding potentially massive seismic disruption. Ninety million cubic meters of earth were moved; 400 contractors and 15,000 workers were employed; a complete infrastructure of roads, camps, airfields, and life-support systems had to be developed; and the logistics effort in bringing men and equipment up from the lower forty-eight states was unprecedented.[14]

Initially, the project was organized on functional lines, with design, procurement, construction, and project control developing the strategic plans, negotiating labor agreements and contracts, developing design options, assuring logistics support, and accomplishing the planning. At a point about 15 percent of the way through construction, however, this organizational configuration changed. The nine-tiered, centralized, functional organization changed to a four-tiered, decentralized, matrix organization (figure 14-4). The result was a highly flexible construction organization relying on a small cadre of senior managers. Emphasis was on leadership, horizontal and informal communication, simple structures and tight reporting relationships—and getting the job done.

The Apollo program also used the same principles of a matrix organization managed by a small program office (figure 14-5), although the implementation of this structural configuration was not phased to the changes in the project life cycle (which is one of the points to be made shortly) since the program office of only about 120 people managed a program that at times consisted of more than 300,000 people.[15]

Acominas is a steel plant recently constructed in Brazil. The story of its organizational development almost mirrors that of TAPS. Like the TAPS schedule, Acominas' project schedule was tight. Constructing the project involved moving 86 million cubic meters of earth, approving half a million drawings, signing 400 contracts, employing a work force of 36,000 people on site, and building a city for 60,000 people for the operation of the plant. The project staff, numbering about 400, was organized on a matrix basis, reporting to an overall project manager (figure 14-6). Like TAPS, Acominas initially was organized along functional lines. Functional managers took the lead in developing the engineering design, planning the project, and negotiating the contracts. As contracts were signed and the project moved into the production phase, however, responsibility was delegated to the project-management teams.[16]

Discussion of the TAPS and Acominas organization development leads to a number of important observations about the organization of projects.

1. The project manager is the single point of integrative responsibility. This idea, which grew out of early studies on reasons for extensive delays in

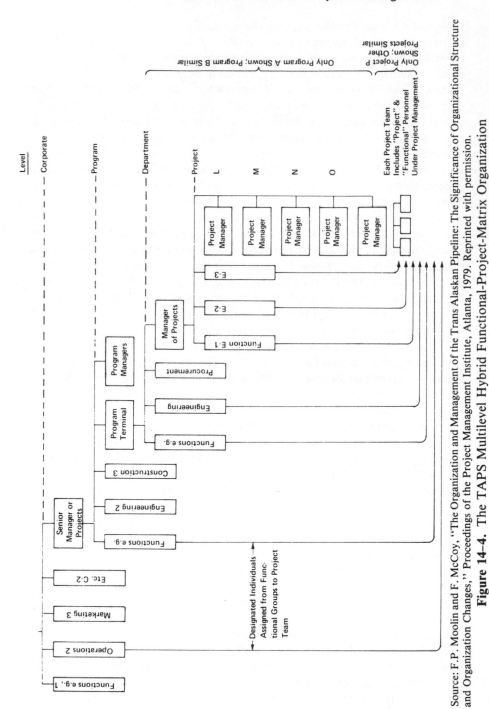

Source: F.P. Moolin and F. McCoy, "The Organization and Management of the Trans Alaskan Pipeline: The Significance of Organizational Structure and Organization Changes," Proceedings of the Project Management Institute, Atlanta, 1979. Reprinted with permission.

Figure 14–4. The TAPS Multilevel Hybrid Functional-Project-Matrix Organization

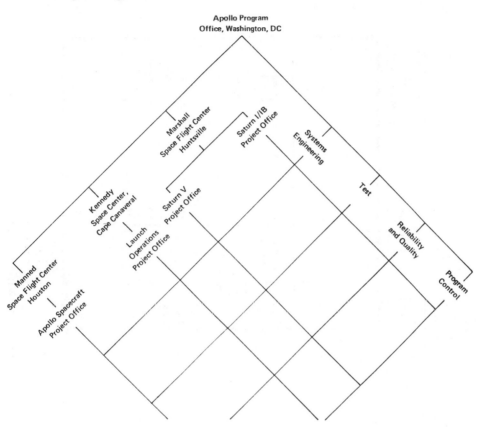

Apollo Program
Office, Washington, DC

Marshall
Space Flight Center
Huntsville

Saturn I/IB
Project Office

Systems
Engineering

Kennedy
Space Center,
Cape Canaveral

Saturn V
Project Office

Test

Launch
Operations
Project Office

Reliability
and Quality

Manned
Space Flight Center
Houston

Apollo Spacecraft
Project Office

Program
Control

Figure 14–5. Apollo Program Organization

U.S. weapons acquisitions programs, proved seminal to the introduction of project-management ideas in the late 1950s and early 1960s. The project manager as the single point of integrative responsibility still remains a core concept, but in the highly complex management environment of both TAPS and Acominas, the concept was implemented in a substantially more subtle way. A number of project or program managers existed, organized hierarchically and often with functional or line managers interspersed. The result—reached independently on projects that were 10,000 miles apart and developed by people in different companies, in different industries, and with no knowledge of the other's organization—is that both superprojects used a hybrid organization that was partly functional, partly project, and largely matrix. Hybrid organizations of this type are unknown in formal management theory.[17]

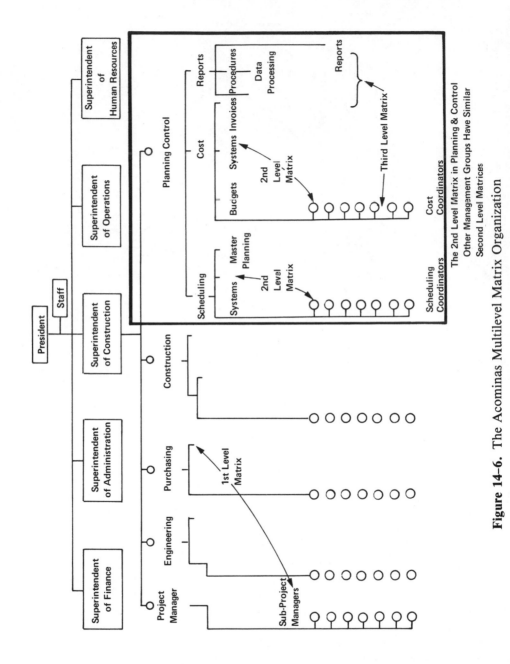

Figure 14–6. The Acominas Multilevel Matrix Organization

2. Typically, large projects require a decentralized, more formal organization during production, with more formal centralization before and after. Both projects exhibited the same pattern of centralization-decentralization-centralization. The great importance of the initial strategic-planning and design phase requires unified direction. This dictates a centralized decision-making process and structure. Later, however, the volume of work and consequent need for coordination expands so greatly that it is impossible to manage with a structure that is so highly centralized. Decision-making resources must be increased or they become overwhelmed; hence, decentralization is in order. Finally, at close-out, the volume of work decreases while the need for unified control (integration with plant start-up) increases. Thus, the organization must return to a more centralized mode.

3. The project organization must change as the needs of the project change. Clearly, as the need for decentralization grows and then lessens, the project organization must adapt. The Acominas matrix was planned to change at the onset of production—about one and a half years after it was set up—which fits with the time usually required to grow a matrix. Initially highly functional, the matrix swung through 45 degrees so that project authority became shared equally with function. On the TAPS project, the change was more sudden, partly because of the greater complexity and schedule urgency of the project. Research suggests that the timing of the project's organization change is determined by the project schedule, whereas the severity of the change (the degree of swing) is a function of the project's size, speed, and complexity.[18]

4. Once decentralized, projects require a substantial management superstructure to effect the necessary coordination. Essentially, projects decentralize because of the pressure on decision-making resources. Once decentralized, however, there is a need for great care and sensitivity in ensuring necessary communication both horizontally and vertically. Informal channels of communication tend to proliferate and become highly important; indeed, this is an aim of the matrix structure. Similarly, there is a profusion of committees and meetings, all largely created to assure the necessary lateral integration. At the same time, however, strict reporting needs and authorization levels must be imposed to ensure that the decentrally made decisions are within the guidelines set out by senior management. Reporting must be by strictly defined cost centers (whose definition should match the work-breakdown structures).

5. In the fast-moving environment of projects, leadership and a mature management style are very important, particularly during the decentralized phase. It is almost self-evident that leadership is vital to project success. Research confirms this.[19] Strong leadership at all levels of management is particularly necessary during the highly interactive decentralized phase. Although conflict tends to be rife throughout the project, it is particularly

evident during production. Therefore, conflict-management techniques become especially important on large projects.[20] Indeed, the successful implementation of both the Acominas and the TAPS organizations depended on behavioral techniques to help implement the required organizational changes and to help managers interact.

6. The project organization must be furnished with independent checks and balances. Conflict should not necessarily be avoided; in fact, it can be genuinely helpful. Both TAPS and Acominas structured planning and control department, independent of the functional and project groups, to provide independent reports on progress. Ideally, the planning and control department should report directly to senior management. Other examples of check-and-balance organization groups found at Acominas and TAPS include quality control, inspection, and auditing.

Conclusion

Project organizations are distinctive forms of organization that move through a defined life cycle. Project management operates at three distinct levels: technical, middle, and senior, and, until recently, too little attention has been paid to the special characteristics of senior project management.

The job of project management is to integrate the work of others toward the project's goal. This requires that management focus on performance at project boundaries and interfaces. The degree of differentiation at an interface, the type of subsystem interdependence, and the need for integration determine the management effort required to achieve integration. The degree of project management required increases with project size, speed, and complexity.

Notes

1. See P.W.G. Morris and S.E. DeLapp, "Managing Change Through Project Management," Proceedings of the Project Management Institute, Atlanta, 1979, for an extended discussion on how project management applies in a wide variety of change situtations.

2. The organic/mechanistic classification comes from T. Burus, and G.M. Stalker, *The Management of Innovation,* (London: Tavistock, 1961).

3. T. Parsons, *Structure and Process in Modern Societies* (Glencoe, Ill.: Free Press, 1960).

4. Unfortunately, this research cited is still classified, but see, for instance, "Financial Status of Major Federal Acquisitions," September 30,

1979 (Washington, D.C.: U.S. General Accounting Office, 1980); L. Merewitz, "How Do Urban Rapid Transit Projects Compare in Cost Estimating Experience?" *Proceedings of the International Conference on Transportation Research,* Bruges, 1973; E. Merrow, S.W. Chapel, and C. Worting, "A Review of Cost Estimation in New Technologies: Implications for Energy Process Plants," R-2481-DOE (Santa Monica: Rand Corporation, July 1979).

5. P. Hall, *Great Planning Disasters* (London: Wiedenfled and Nicolson, 1980).

6. See, for instance, Hall, *Great Planning Disasters;* L. Wynant, "Essential Elements of Project Financing," *Harvard Business Review,* May–June 1980; "U.S. Builders Prepare for Superprojects," *Business Week,* September 26, 1977.

7. M. Horwitch, "Managing a Colossus," *Wharton Magazine,* Summer 1979, pp. 34–41.

8. See, for instance, T. Wolfe, *The Right Stuff* (New York: Farrar, Strauss and Giroux, 1979); R. Seamans, Jr., and F.I. Ordway, "The Apollo Tradition: An Object Lesson for the Management of Large-Scale Technological Endeavors," *Interdisciplinary Science Reviews* 2 (1977):270–304.

9. H. Minitzberg, *Structuring of Organizations* (Englewood Cliffs, N.J.: Prentice-Hall, 1979).

10. E.M. Miller, "Technology, Territory and Time: The Internal Differentiation of Complex Production Systems," *Human Relations* 12 (1959):243–273.

11. P.R. Lawrence and J.W. Lorsch, *Organization and Environment: Managing Differentiation and Integration* (Cambridge, Mass.: Harvard University Press, 1967).

12. J.D. Thompson, *Organizations in Action* (New York: McGraw-Hill, 1967).

13. This list is based on J.R. Galbraith *Organization Design* (Reading, Mass.: Addison-Wesley, 1973).

14. See, for instance, F.P. Moolin and F. McCoy, "The Organization and Management of the Trans Alaskan Pipeline: The Significance of Organizational Structure and Organization Changes," Proceedings of the Project Management Institute, Atlanta, 1979.

15. See, for instance, J.S. Baumgartner, *Systems Management* (Washington, D.C.: Bureau of National Affairs, 1979), pp. 13–25.

16. E. Reis de Carvalho and P.W.G. Morris, "Project Matrix Organizations, Or How To Do the Matrix Swing," Proceedings of the Project Management Institute, Los Angeles, 1978.

17. P. Davis and P.R. Lawrence *Matrix* (Reading, Mass.: Addison-Wesley, 1977).

18. P.W.G. Morris, "An Organizational Analysis of Project Management in the Building Industry," *Build International* 6 (1971).

19. D.C. Murphy, B.N. Baker, and D. Fisher, "Determinants of Project Success," Boston College School of Management, 1976.

20. H.L. Thamhain, and D.L. Wilemon, "Conflict Management in Project Life Cycles," *Sloan Management Review,* Summer 1975.

Appendix 14A:
Project-Management Phases
in Various Management
Situations

Project Phases	Project Situations		
	New Venture	*Turnaround*	*Motion Picture*
Objective	Successfully launch a new venture (business, product, etc.)	Within a defined time period, turn a poor performance situation into a successful one	Make a movie
Strategy and plans	Strategy for: Financing venture Product Marketing Plans for: Financing Production Marketing/sales Maintenance	Strategy for: Capitalizing on existing strengths Investment of resources Plans for: Investment Staff utilization Performance schedule and major review points	Strategy for: Financing production Casting Artistic content Plans for: Script Shooting schedule Distribution Overall Production
Organization	Transition organization Organization development Liaison with major technical, financial, and marketing groups Objective organization Operate venture after start-up	Transition organization Requires clearly defined charter and control over resources Establish objective organization Objective organization Assume operations after turnaround complete	Core production organization Develop strategy Initial plans for script and cast Support organization Shooting Editing Overall production Objective organization Distribution

Control	Control of: Technical performance Operational preparedness of back-up units Schedule progress Costs Revenues projections	Control of: Financial investment and projected revenue Technical performance Technical resources and personnel employed Key schedule events and milestones	Control of: Cash, budget, costs Shooting schedule Staffing schedule Props, wardrobe, etc.
Implementation	Coordination with support units must be maintained Transition from development to operation is critical	Establish esprit de corps among transition staff Ensure acceptance by other organization staff members Closely track performance with schedule	Ensure good relations with unions, actors, and agents, production staff, financiers Balance production schedule and costs with expected revenues

Project Situations

Project Phases	R&D	Electioneering	Urban Development	Organization Change
Objective	Conduct research and into a marketable product	Obtain the election of a candidate	Develop and implement an urban development program	Effect a change in structure, staffing, systems, or style in an organization
Strategy and plans	Strategy for: Investment Timing Research direction Plans for: Staffing Investment Review points	Strategy for: Financing campaign Securing key support Presentation to electorate Voters to target Plans for: Fund raising Securing endorsements Presentation of issues and media use	Strategy for: Financing development Political approval Marketing Plans for: Financing Political approval Construction phasing Land acquisition	Strategy for: Investment Timing Plans for: Commitment by key staff Organizational units to be included Implementation of the change
Organization	Transition organization R&D group maintain linkages with marketing and other groups No objective organization	Transition organization Coordination between professional and volunteer campaigners Secure additional workers—individuals and groups Objective organization Only if election is successful	Transition organization Planning/Design Political liaison Construction Marketing Objective organization Property management	Transition organization Core group to interface with all affected groups Plan for transition to objective organization Objective organization Assume control after complete

Control	Control of:
	Technical progress
	Costs
	Revenue forecasts
	
	Schedules for each phase and linkage between phases
		Control of:
		Expenditures
		Funds raised
		Voter-support
		    projections
			Control of:
			Funding commitments
			Leasing/selling
			Cash receipts/Disburse-
			    ments
			Construction progress
			Development approval
			Land purchase
				Control of
				Schedule
				Costs
				
				Technical progress

Implementation	Must ensure continuous linkages between research and development functions Go/no-go decision on development is critical and requires input from other units in organization	Rapid build-up of organization requires close coordination of numerous individuals Fund raising and expenditure must be closely matched	Achieve and retain political support from elected officials and residents Balance construction rate, financing, and sales	Commitment required from key leaders followed by all affected persons Management of potential conflicts as change occurs

Project Phases	Project Situations					
	Rural Development	Management Consulting	Construction	Aerospace	Shipbuilding	Weapons
Objective	Develop and implement a rural-development program	Counsel on a management issue or issues	Design and construct a physical facility	Design and manufacture an aerospace product	Design and build a ship	Develop and manufacture a weapons system
Strategy and plans	Strategy for: Financing development, Social development, Technical approach; Plans for: Financing, Social development, Technical development, Implementation	Strategy for: Approach to issue, Staffing, Approach to client; Plans for: Work schedule, Deliverables, Staffing	Strategy for: Financing, Contracting, Technical specifications; Plans for: Financing, Schedule, Technical development, Contracting, Sale/transfer			
Organization	Transition organization, Interface with government, residents, social agencies, etc.	Transition organization, Maintain relations with client, Coordinate among consulting staff, No objectiv organization	Transition organization, Coordination of contractors, Liaison with future users, government, etc., Transfer to owner/user/client, No objective organization			

	Objective organization Post development social organization to continue to deal with social impacts		
Control	Control of: Technical progress Schedule Costs Funding	Control of: Costs Technical progress Deliverable schedule	Control of: Technical progress Schedule Costs Revenue
Implementation	Monitor and ameliorate impact of social and finan- cial disruptions	Must have constant focus on end objectives and status of work to date to ensure product meets re- quirements Expenditures must be matched to progress so overruns do not occur	Coordination of a great number of organizations and individuals to ensure schedule completion Control expenditures to avoid overruns

Source: P.W.G. Morris and S.E. DeLapp, "Managing Change Through Project Management," Proceedings of the Project Management Institute, Atlanta, 1979. Reprinted with permission.

15 The Human Side of Project Management

David I. Cleland

Taken in its cultural context, project management is a complex whole that includes knowledge, belief, skills, attitudes, and other capabilities and habits acquired by people who are members of some project society. An organization that develops maturity in the art and science of project management exhibits some distinctive cultural characteristics, which begin to emerge when the project-driven matrix comes into play.

The Nature of a Business Culture

The word *culture* is being used more and more in the lexicon of management to describe the ambience of a business organization. The culture associated with each organization has several distinctive characteristics that differentiate the company from others. In the IBM Corporation, for example, the simple precept "IBM means service" sets the tone for the entire organization, infusing all aspects of its environment and generating its distinctive culture. At 3M, the motto "Never kill a new product idea" creates an organizational atmosphere of inventiveness and creativity. In some large corporations, such as Hewlett-Packard, General Electric, and Johnson & Johnson, the crucial parts of the organization are kept small to encourage a local culture, which, in turn, encourages a personal touch in the context of a motivated, entrepreneurial spirit of teamwork.

Understanding the culture of the organization is a prerequisite to introducing project management. An organization's culture reflects the composite management style of its executives, a style that has much to do with the organization's ability to adapt to such a change as the introduction of a project-management system.

In the preparation of this chapter, the author has drawn heavily from "The Cultural Ambience of Matrix Management," *Management Review,* November 1981; copyright 1981 by Amacom, a division of the American Management Associations. All rights reserved. Reprinted with permission.

The Roots of the Matrix Organization

The cultural ambience of the project-driven matrix organization is unique in many respects. It should not be strange to us, however, since our first organization, the family, has key features of the matrix design. In the traditional family unit, the child is responsible to and has authority exercised over him by two superiors (parents). A perceptive child soon learns that he must work out major decisions and such matters with both his bosses. If his parents have agreed on a work-breakdown structure in which each will exercise authority and assume responsibility over a particular aspect of raising the child, it will be easier for him to get along with them and with his peer group. A child may have to find ways to collaborate with both parents as well as with his siblings and peers, adjusting to all groups.

When the child goes to school, a similar matrix design is found. The student is placed in a homeroom, with a teacher whose main business is administration, logistics support, and discipline. The student is taught by other teachers, who are the functional specialists. Thus, the student has several more superiors to whom he is accountable, as well as a larger peer group. If the student is active in extracurricular activities, still more bosses come into his life. Success and acceptance in these activities generally require peer acceptance, teamwork, and an ability to communicate with his superiors and his peers.

When the student leaves school and seeks employment, he may find a more hierarchical structure, yet the new matrix is in many ways similar to those already experienced. If his initial job is on a production line, the production foreman becomes boss number one, yet the quality-control specialist can shut down the production line. The perceptive individual finds that certain staff specialists (personnel, finance, maintenance, wage and salary) and even informal leaders in the peer groups temper the sovereign domain of the foreman. He soon finds that certain people in the organization exercise power simply because they have control of information (such as the production control specialist) or have become experts in some areas. People look to the expert to make decisions and to take a leadership role in certain matters. The role of the union steward as a tempering influence on production techniques and policies soon become obvious to the worker. If he is active in community affairs, he finds many other bosses telling him (or suggesting) what to do. Who, then, is really the boss? It depends on the situation—just as it does in the matrix organization.

Thus, the sharing context of project management should not be foreign to any of us, as our family life, education, and work experience have given us ample exposure to working for and satisfying several bosses and learning to communicate and work with peers. Why, then, is there such resistance to matrix design? I believe the resistance has its roots in several cultural factors. One such factor is the concept that authority flows from the top of the organization down through a chain of command. Ecclesiastical organizations have contributed much to organization theory, and many of these contributions have reinforced the vertical structure. Have we not always assumed that heaven—by whatever name it is called—is a higher place or state? The Bible speaks of ascending into heaven—why not moving to heaven on a lateral basis?

A good friend of mine who is a competent minister once delivered a sermon on the theme that hell was a state of mind, not a place. After the sermon, I questioned whether, if hell is a state of mind and not a place, it follows that heaven is a state of mind and not a place. He said, "Perhaps, but we are not ready for that yet." Like heaven, perhaps the matrix organization is more a state of mind than anything else.

No one would doubt the strong influence the Bible has had on our thinking. Indeed, the words of St. Matthew are familiar: "No man can serve two masters: for either he will hate the one, and love the other; or else he will hold to the one, and despise the other" (Matthew 6:24). Part of the rationalization for the principle of unity of command may well be traced back to this verse. In managerial theory, this principle and its corolaries— parity of authority and responsibility; compulsory staff advice; line commands, staff advises; span of control; and so forth—provide the conceptual foundation for the hierarchical organizational form. Indeed, managers and professionals often have asked, "How can I work for two bosses?" Matthew also provides us with the basis for doing so: "Render therefore unto Ceasar the things which are Caesar's; and unto God the things that are God's" (Matthew 22:21).

I contend that, in the light of both pragmatic and cultural experience, there is as much basis for the matrix design, with its multidimensional sharing of authority, responsibility, accountability, and results, as there is for the hierarchical style of management.

The Matrix Organizational Design

I use the concept of organizational design in a broad context to include organizational structure, management systems and processes, formal and informal interpersonal relationships, and motivational patterns. The matrix design is a compromise between a bureaucratic approach that is too inflexible and a simple unit structure that is too centralized. The design is fluid; personnel assignments, authority bases, and interpersonal relationships are constantly shifting. It combines a sense of democracy within a bureaucratic context.

From an organizational-design viewpoint, the entire organization must be psychologically attuned to results—the accomplishments within the organization that support higher-level organizational objectives, goals, and strategies. The purpose of a matrix design is not only to get the best from its strong project approach and strong functional approach but to complement these by a strong unity of command at the senior level, to insure that the source of power is maintained in the organization. In some companies, only one or a few divisions might require a realignment to the project-driven matrix form; the others might be left in the pyramidal, hierarchical form. Indeed, a single organization chart cannot realistically portray the maze of relationships that exist inside a large organization, because some elements select project management, others opt for the conventional line-staff design, and still others choose some hybrid form.

The matrix organizational design is result-oriented and information-related. The design implies that there is a need for someone who can manage a process of cutting across the line functions. A compromise results through the bipolarity of functional specialization and project integration. Out of the lateral relations—direct contact, liaison roles, and integration—comes a faculty to make and implement decisions and to process information without overburdening the hierarchical communication channels. It is the need to reduce the decision process on the hierarchical channels that motivates the formal undertaking of lateral relations through establishing a bilateral design: (1) project managers, who are responsible for results, and (2) functional managers, who are responsible for providing resources to attain results.

When implementing a matrix design in the early stages, there usually is poor harmony between behavioral reality and the structural form. At this stage, the process of integration becomes important, and a series of critical actions must be initiated and monitored by senior management. Superior-subordinate relationships need to be modified; individual self-motivation leading to peer acceptance becomes critical. The development of strategies for dealing with conflict, the encouragement of participation techniques, and the delineation of expected authority and responsibility patterns are crucial. The complexity of the resulting organizational design, described by Peter Drucker as "fiendishly difficult," reminds us that the matrix design should be used only when there is no suitable alternative. The design lacks the simplicity of the conventional hierarchy. The different nature of a project in the various stages of its life cycle creates a lack of stability. Key people on the project team must know not only their specialties but also how those specialties contribute to the whole. The emphasis must be on flexibility, peer informality, and minimization of hierarchy. To change an existing design to a fully functioning matrix form takes time, however—perhaps several years.

The matrix organizational design is the most complex form of organizational alignment that can be used. The integration of specialists and supporting staff into a project team requires strong and continuing collaborative effort, and the coordination of effort in such a design requires a continuing integration of the mutual efforts of the team members. Authority (and, consequently, power) tend to flow to the individual who has the needed information and whose particular skills and knowledge are necessary to make a decision. Many managers are found in the matrix design: project managers, functional managers, work-package managers, general managers, staff managers. The greater the number of project teams, the greater the number of managers that will be used. As a result, the management costs are increased in such an organizational approach.

The introduction of project management into an organization tends to change established management practice with respect to such matters as authority and responsibility, procedural arrangements, support systems, department specialization, span of control, resource-allocation patterns, establishment of priorities, and evaluation of people. Performance goals within such organizations tend to be assigned in terms of the interfunctional flow of work needed to support a project. When this is done, established work groups within the functional agencies are often disrupted. In addition, there is a potential for the staffing pattern to involve duplication. The functional manager previously had the freedom to manage the organization in a relatively unilateral fashion, for he carried out integration himself or a higher authority handled it. Now he is forced into an interface in an environment that places a premium on the integration of resources through a project-team consensus in order to accomplish project results. He must learn to work with a vocal and demanding horizontal organization.

The cultural characteristic of the matrix design causes two key attitudes to emerge: the manager who realizes that authority has its limits and the professional who recognizes that authority has its place.

The Cultural Ambience

In its organizational context, a cultural ambience for matrix management deals with the social expression manifest within the organization when it is engaged in managing projects. A cultural system emerges that reflects certain behavioral patterns characteristic of all the members of that organization. This system influences the skills, knowledge, and value systems of the people who are the primary organizational clientele. The clientele are those who have some vested interest in the success of an organizational effort.

Thus, the primary project clientele include the managers and professionals in the organizational society who are collectively sharing the authority and responsibility for completing a project on time and within budget—

the superiors, subordinates, peers, and associates who work together to bring the project to a successful completion. The cultural ambience that ultimately emerges is dependent on the way these primary clientele feel and act in their professional roles, both on the project team and within the larger organizational context. The integration of these clientele results in an ambience that has the following characteristics: organizational openness; participation; increased human problems; consensus decision making; objective merit evaluation; new criteria for wage and salary classification; new career paths; acceptable adversary roles; organizational flexibility; improvement in productivity; increased innovation; and realignment of supporting systems.

Organizational Openness

A propensity toward organizational openness is one of the most characteristic attributes of the matrix design. This openness is demonstrated through a receptiveness to new ideas and a sharing of information and problems by the peer group. Newcomers to a matrix organization typically are accepted without any concern. There is a willingness to share organizational challenges and frustrations with the newcomers. This characteristic openness of project-team management was described in one company as "no place to hide in the organization."[1]

Participation

Participation in the project-driven matrix organization calls for new behavior, attitudes, skills, and knowledge. The demands of working successfully in the matrix design create opportunities for the people as well as for the organization. For the people, there are more opportunities to attract attention and to try their mettle as potential future managers. Because matrix management increases the amount and the pattern of recurring contracts between individuals, communication is more intense. The resolution of conflict is also more intense than in the traditional organization, in which conflict can be resolved by talking to the functional boss. In a matrix design, at least two bosses must become involved—the manager who provides the resources and the manager who is held accountable for results. As a last resort, these two managers, if locked in conflict, may appeal to the common line supervisor for resolution. Matrix management demands higher levels of collaboration. In order to have collaboration, however, trust and commitment are needed on the part of the individuals in the organization. They must take personal risks in sharing information and revealing their own views, attitudes, and feelings.

There is growing evidence that individuals today wish to influence their work situation and to create a democratic environment at their places of work. People expect variety in their organizational life-style as well as in their private lives. The flexibility and openness of the matrix design can accommodate these demands.

The degree to which people are committed to participate openly and fully in matrix-organization effort can influence results. In a study of more than 650 projects, including 200 variables, Murphy, Baker, and Fisher, found that certain variables were associated with the perceived failure of projects. Lack of team participation in decision making and problem solving was one important variable associated with perceived project failure. In contrast, project-team participation in setting schedules and budgets was significantly related to project success.[2]

Increased Human Problems

Reeser conducted research at several aerospace companies to examine the question of whether project organization has a built-in capacity to cause some real human problems of its own.[3] His research findings suggested that insecurity about possible unemployment, career retardation, and personal development is considered a more significant problem by subordinates in project organizations than by subordinates in functional organizations. Reeser noted that project subordinates can easily be frustrated by make-work assignments, ambiguity, and conflict in the work environment. Project subordinates tend to have less loyalty to the organization, and there are frustrations because of having more than one boss. The central implication of Reeser's findings is that, although there may be persuasive justifications for using a matrix design, relief from human problems is not one of them.

Even with formal definition of organizational roles, the shifting of people between projects does have some noticeable effects. People may feel insecure, for example, if they are not provided ongoing career counseling. In addition, the shifting of people from project to project may interfere with some of the basic training of employees and the executive development of salaried personnel. This neglect can hinder the growth and development of people in their respective fields.

Consensus Decision Making

Many people are involved in making decisions. Members of the matrix team actively contribute in defining questions or problems as well as in designing courses of action to resolve problems and develop opportunities in the management of effort. Professionals who become members of a matrix team gain added influence in the organization as they become associated with important decisions supporting an effort. They tend to become more closely associated with the decision makers, both within the organization and outside. Perceptive professionals readily recognize how their professional lives are broadened.

A series of documents that describe the formal authority and responsibility for decision making of key project clientele should be developed for the organization. If a manager is accustomed to a clear line of authority to make unilateral decisions, the participation of team members in the project decision process makes management more complex. The result is worth the effort, however, for the decisions tend to be of higher quality. Also, by participating in the decision process, people have a high degree of commitment to carrying out the decision effectively.

Objective Merit Evaluation

This is an important area of concern to the individual in the matrix design. If the individual finds himself working for two bosses (the functional or work-package manager and the project manager), chances are that both will evaluate his merit and promotion fitness. Usually, the functional manager initiates the evaluation; then the project manager concurs in the evaluation with a suitable endorsement. If the two evaluators are unable to agree on the evaluation, it can be referred to a third party for resolution. Individuals who are so rated usually favor such a procedure, as it reinforces their membership on the project team and insures that an equitable evaluation is given. A project-team member who has been assigned to the team from a functional organization may find himself away from the daily supervision of his functional supervisor. Under such circumstances, a fair and objective evaluation might not be feasible. By having the project manager participate in the evaluation, objectivity and equity are maintained.

New Criteria for Wage and Salary Classification

The executive rank and salary classification of a project manager will vary depending on the requirements of his position, the importance of the project to the company, and the like. Most organizations adopt a policy of paying competitive salaries. The typical salary-classification schema, however, is based on the number and grade of managers and professionals that the executive supervises. In the management of a project, although the project manager may supervise only two or three people on his staff, he is still responsible for bringing the project in on time and at the budgeted cost. In so doing, he is responsible for managing the efforts of many others who do not report to him in the traditional sense. Therefore, new criteria are required for determining the salary level of a project manager. Organizations with successful salary-classification schema for project managers' salaries have used such criteria as the following:

1. Duration of the project
2. Importance of the project to the company
3. Importance of the customer
4. Annual project dollars
5. Payroll and level of the people who report directly to the project manager (staff)
6. Payroll and level of the people with whom the project manager must interface directly on a continuing basis
7. Complexity of the project requirements
8. Complexity of the project
9. Complexity of project interfaces
10. Payroll and rank of the individual to whom the project manager reports
11. Potential payoff of the project
12. Pressures the project manager is expected to face

In many companies, the use of project management is still in its adolescence, and suitable salary criteria have not been determined. In such cases, it is not uncommon to find individuals designated as project managers who are not coded as managerial personnel in the salary-classification and executive-rank criteria. Word of this may get around, and the individual's authority might be compromised. I have found this situation arising usually because of failure of the wage and salary staff specialists to develop suitable criteria for adjusting the salary grade of the project managers. This problem is not so significant in industries wherein project management is a way of life, such as aerospace and construction.

New Career Paths

The aspiring individual typically has two career paths open to him: remaining as a manager in his technical field or seeking a general-manager position. Alternatively, he may prefer to remain a professional in his field and become a senior advisor—for example, a senior engineer. Project management opens up another field in management. The individual who is motivated to enter management ranks can seek a position as project manager of a small project and can use this as a stepping-stone to higher-level management positions. It is an excellent way to learn the job of a general manager, since the job of project manager is much like that of a general manager, except that the project manager usually does not have the formal legal authority of the general manager. This should not deter the project manager; rather, it should motivate him to develop his persuasive and other interpersonal and negotiation skills—necessary skills for success in general management.

Acceptable Adversary Roles

An adversary role emerges in project management as the primary project clientele find that participation in the key decisions and problems is socially acceptable. An adversary role may be assumed by any of the project clientele who sense that something is wrong in the management of the project. Such an adversary role questions goals, strategies, and objectives and asks the tough questions that have to be asked. Such a spontaneous adversary role provides a valuable check to guard against decisions that are unrealistic or overly optimistic. A socially acceptable adversary role facilitates the rigorous and objective development of data bases on which decisions are made. The prevailing culture in an organization, however, may discourage the individual from playing the adversary role that will help management comprehend the reality of a situation. This circumstance is possible in all hierarchical institutions.

An adversary role presumes that upward communication of ideas and concerns is encouraged. As people actively participate in the project deliberations, they are quick to suggest innovative ideas for improving the project or to sound the alarm when things do not seem to be going as they should. If the adversary role is not present—perhaps because its emergence is inhibited by the management style of the principal managers—information concerning potential organizational failures will not surface.

An example of such stifling of the adversary role is found in the case of a company involved in managing an urban-transportation project. In the late 1960s, this company attempted to grow from a $250 million per year subcontractor in the aerospace industry into a producer of ground-transit equipment. In pursuing this strategy, it won prime contracts for two large urban-rail systems. Heavy losses in its rail programs put the company into financial difficulties. What went wrong?

The company got into difficulty partly because the chief executive dominated the other company executives, even though he was unable to face overriding practical considerations. When major projects in the rail-systems business were in difficulty, the unrealistic optimism demonstrated by the chief executive prevented any other executive from doing much about it. In the daily staff meetings, the executives quickly learned that any negative or pessimistic report on a project would provoke open and sharp criticism from the chief executive. Project managers quickly learned that, in the existing cultural ambience, bringing bad news would not be tolerated. Consequently, they glossed over problem areas and emphasized the positive in order to please him.

On one of their large contracts, they submitted a bid that was 23 percent below the customer's own estimate and $11 million under the next lowest competitive bid. The project manager had thought that this estimate was too low but had not argued against it because he did not want to express a negative minority view when he was in charge of the program. The cultural ambience within this company during this period might be summarized as follows: Don't tell the boss any bad news—only report good news; if you bring bad news, you run the risk of being sharply criticized.

Members of a project team must feel free to ask tough questions during the life of the project. When the members of a team can play an adversary role, a valuable check-and-balance mechanism exists to guard against unrealistic decisions. Within Texas Instruments, for example, a cultural ambience exists wherein an adversary role can emerge. Consequently, "It is impossible to bury a mistake in this company. The grass roots of the corporation are visible from the top . . . the people work in teams and that results in a lot of peer pressure and peer recognition.[4]

Organizational Flexibility

The lines of authority and responsibility defining the organizational structure tend to be flexible in the matrix organization. There is much give and take across these lines, with people assuming an organizational role that the situation warrants rather than what the position description says should be done. Authority in such an organizational context gravitates to the person who has the best credentials to make the required judgment.

The matrix design provides a vehicle for maximum organizational flexibility; no one has tenure on a matrix team. There are variable tasks that people perform, a change in the type of situations they may be working on, and an ebb and flow of workloads as the work of the organization fluctuates. When an individual's skills are no longer needed on a team, he can be assigned back to his permanent functional home.

There are some inherent problems in the flexibility of the matrix organization, however. The need for staffing tends to be more variable. Both the quantity and the quality of needed personnel are difficult to estimate because of the various projects that are going on in the organization. A structural-design group, for example, may have a surplus of design engineers who are not assigned to any one project at a particular time. The manpower estimates for coming projects, however, may indicate that these professionals will be needed for project assignments in several months. A functional structural-design manager has the choice of whether to release the engineers and reduce his overhead or to assign them to make-work for the period and forgo the future costs of recruitment, selection, and training. The same manager may anticipate assigning these professionals to an emerging project, but, if the emerging project is delayed, or canceled, the project manager may not need the people for some time.

As the work effort nears its end and perceptive individuals begin to look for other jobs, there can be a reduction in their output level. This reduction can damage the efficacy with which the project is being managed. Paradoxically, although morale takes on added significance in the matrix team, the design itself may result in lowering it. Thus, the organizational flexibility of project management creates some problems as well as opportunities.

Improvement in Productivity

Texas Instruments attributes productivity improvement in the company to the use of project teams. Its productivity improvement over the past years has slightly more than offset the combined impact of its wage and benefit increases (averaging 9.2 percent annually) and its price decreases (averaging 6.4 percent per unit).[5]

At Texas Instruments, more than 83 percent of employees are organized into people-involvement teams, seeking ways to improve their own productivity. The company views its people as interchangeable—"like auto parts." The culture there is much like that of Japanese companies—a strong spirit of belonging, a strong work ethic, competitive zeal, company loyalty, and rational decision making. The culture of Texas Instruments "has its roots buried deep in a soil of Texas' pioneer work ethic, dedication, toughness and tenacity—it (the culture) is a religion. The climate polarizes people—either you are incorporated into the culture or rejected."[6]

The experience of Litton Industries' Microwave Cooking Division shows that the use of project teams in the manufacturing function has increased productivity. Since the manufacturing organization was grouped into team units, production increased fourfold in fifteen months. Product quality has increased, 1,000 new production workers have been added to a base of 400 people, and unit production costs have declined 10 percent to 15 percent.[7] Some other claims of productivity increases that have come to my attention are as follows:[8] A steel-company chief executive states: "Properly applied, 'matrix' management improves profitability because it allows progress to be made on a broader front; with a given staff size, i.e., more programs and projects simultaneously pursued (including those concerning productivity)." The chief executive of a company in the microprocessor industry declares that the company's success (15 percent of the microprocessor market, $1.8 million in revenue, 18.1 percent return on investment) would not be possible without matrix management. A chemical company president claims: "Matrix management improves people productivity." The experiences of these companies suggest that project-management techniques can assist in raising productivity.

Increased Innovation

In the private sector, in industries with a fast-changing state of the art, product innovation is critical for survival. There is evidence that the use of project teams has helped to further innovation within such organizations. Project teams are used successfully, for example, in the aerospace industry, where the ability to innovate is essential, particularly in the development and production of sophisticated weaponry.

Why does a project team seem to foster innovation in organizations? Innovation comes about because an individual has an idea—a technological or market idea—and surrounds himself with some people who believe in the idea and are committed to it. A small team is formed of people who become advocates and missionaries for the idea. The team of people represents a diverse set of disciplines that view the idea differently. It is difficult to hide anything in such an environment. The openness, the freedom of expression, and the need to demonstrate personal effectiveness all seem to be conducive to the creativity necessary to innovate. Within such organizations, decision making tends to be by consensus. An element of esprit de corps exists. The creativity and the innovative characteristics of small teams is well illustrated by the Texas Instrument situation.[9]

Texas Instruments has been extremely successful in using teams. The company has more than 200 product-consumer centers (PCC), in each of which the manager runs a small business of his or her own with responsibilities that include both long-term and short-term considerations. These managers have access to functional groups and are able to use the enormous resources of the functional organization. Thus, the entrepreneur—the innovator—can flourish by having available the technical resources that are needed to do the job.

Project teams that are used effectively can take advantage of the scale economies of large organizations, but, by their team nature, the flexibility of a small, innovative organization is realized. An early research effort in the use of program (project) organizations noted that such organizations seemed to have been more successful in developing and introducing new products than have businesses without program organizations.[10]

L.W. Ellis, director of research at International Telephone and Telegraph Corporation, claims that temporary groups (project teams) that are well organized and have controlled autonomy can stimulate innovation by overcoming resistance to change. Cross-functional and diagonal communication within the project team and with outside interested parties helps to reduce resistance to change.[11]

Jermakowicz found that the matrix design was the most effective of the three major organizational forms he studied in insuring the implementation or introduction of new projects, while a pure project organization produced the most creative solutions.[12]

Kolodny, reporting on a study of his own and also citing some other studies, comments on the effect that matrix organizations have on new-product innovation.[13] He cites Davis and Lawrence, who point to an apparent high correlation between matrix organizational designs and very high rates of new-product innovation.[14] In his summary, Kolodny also notes that there is an apparent relationship between high rates of new-product innovation, as measured by the successful introduction of new products, and matrix organizational designs.[15]

There is no question that an organization whose business involves the work of temporary projects is more anxiety-ridden, tension-filled, and demanding of personal competence and equilibrium than a stable, conventionally organized one. The matrix design is complex, but its successful operation reflects a complementary mode of collaborative relationships in an open ambience. It is an adaptive, rapidly changing temporary management system that can favorably influence organizational innovation.

Realignment of Support Systems

As the use of project management grows in an organization, it soon becomes apparent that many of the systems that have been organized on a traditional, hierarchical basis need to be realigned to support the project team. What initially appears to be only an organizational change soon becomes something larger. Effective project management requires timely and relevant information on the project; accordingly, the information systems must be modified to accommodate the project manager's needs. Financial and accounting systems, project planning and control techniques, personnel evaluations, and other support systems also require adjustment to meet project-management needs.

Development of General Management Attitudes

An organizational culture is, in a sense, the aggregate of individual values, attitudes, beliefs, prejudices, and social standards. A change for the individuals means cultural changes. The matrix design, when properly applied, tends to provide more opportunity to more people to act in a general-manager mode. With this kind of general-manager thinking, the individual is able to contribute more to organizational decision making and information processing.

The matrix design, with its openness and demands for persuasive skills, provides an especially good environment for the manager-to-be to test his ability to make things happen by the strength of persuasive and negotiative powers. A perceptive general manager knows that little is accomplished solely by virtue of his hierarchical position; a great deal depends on his ability to persuade others to his way of thinking. Exposure to the workings and ambience of the matrix culture brings this point home clearly and succinctly.

Effective collaboration on a project team requires a great deal of a needed ingredient—trust. To develop this trust, individuals must be prepared to take personal risks in sharing resources, information, views, prejudices, attitudes, and feelings to act democratically. Not everyone can do that, but executives in successful companies are able to do so. In the Digital Equipment Corporation, for example, where a matrix environment prevails, the ambience is described as "incredibly democratic" but not for everyone. Many technical people cannot stand the lack of structure and the indefiniteness. In such an organization, bargaining skills are essential to survival.[16] The matrix design is permanent; the deployment of people is changing constantly. In such a transitional situation, the only things that prevent breakdown are the personal relationships as conflicts are resolved and personnel assignments are changed. Communication is needed continually to maintain the interpersonal relationships and to stimulate people to contribute to the project-team efforts.

Some Warnings and Guidelines

The matrix organizational design is difficult to get started and challenging to operate. The more conventional the culture has been, the more challenges will emerge in moving to the matrix form. A few caveats and guidelines are in order for those who plan to initiate and use a project-driven matrix design.

1. Realize that strategic patience is absolutely necessary. It takes time to change the systems and the people who make the matrix work.

2. Promote, by word and example, an open and flexible attitude in the organization. Encourage the notion that change is inevitable and that a free exchange of ideas is necessary to make project management work.

3. Develop a scheme for organizational objectives, goals, and strategies that will provide the framework for an emerging project-management culture.

4. Accept the idea that some people may never be able to adjust to the unstructured, democratic ambience of the matrix culture. For these people, a place in the organization must be assured wherein they can remain insulated from the difficult surroundings of the matrix organization.

5. Be mindful of the tremendous importance that team commitment plays in managing project activities. Make use of the philosophy of a winning football team—the commitment to win is an absolute prerequisite to becoming a championship team.

6. Provide a forum whereby conflict can be resolved before it deteriorates into interpersonal strife.

7. Realize that project management is not a panacea for organic organizational maladies. In fact, the implementing of a project-management system will bring to light many organizational problems and opportunities that have remained hidden in the conventional line-and-staff organization.

8. Be aware that the particular route an organization follows in its journey to the matrix design must evolve from the existing culture.

9. Recognize that senior-management support and commitment are essential to success.

10. Work for communication within the company that is uninhibited, thorough, and complete. Information requirements for project management require definition. Individuals who have a need to know must have access to the information necessary to do their job. Those in key positions must be able to understand and use the project-generated information.

11. Be aware that shifting to a matrix form is easier for a younger organization. For large, well-established companies in which a rigid bureaucracy endures, the shift will be formidable.

12. Institute a strong educational effort to acquaint key managers and professionals with the theory and practice of project management. Time should be taken to do this at the beginning, using the existing culture as a point of departure.

Summary

The real culture of project management refers to actual behavior—the factors and events that really exist in the life of an organization. The introduction of project management into an existing culture will set into motion a system of effects that will change attitudes, values, beliefs, and management systems to a participative, democratic mode. Thus, a new cultural context for the sharing of decisions, results, rewards, and accountability ultimately will emerge as an organization matures in the use of project management.

Notes

1. "Texas Instruments Shows U.S. Business How to Survive in the 1980's," *Business Week,* September 18, 1978, pp. 66–92.

2. D.C. Murphy, Bruce N. Baker, and Delmar Fisher, "Determinants of Project Success" (Springfield, Va.: National Technical Information Services, 1974), Accession No. N–74–30392, p. 60669.

3. Clayton Reeser, "Some Potential Human Problems of the Project Form of Organization," *Academy of Management Journal* 12 (December 1979).

4. "Texas Instruments Shows U.S. Business."

5. Ibid.

6. Ibid.

7. William W. George, "Task Teams for Rapid Growth," *Harvard Business Review,* March-April 1977, p. 71.

8. These are productivity claims cited to the author in correspondence.

9. See "Texas Instruments Shows U.S. Business."

10. E.R. Corey and S.H. Starr, *Organization Strategy: A Marketing Approach,* chapter 6 (Boston: Division of Research, Harvard Business School, 1970).

11. L.W. Ellis, "Effective Use of Temporary Groups for New Product Development," *Research Management,* January 1979, pp. 31–34.

12. Wladyslaw Jermakowicz, "Organizational Structures in the R&D Sphere," *R&D Management,* No. 8 (Special Issue), 1978, pp. 107–113.

13. Harvey F. Kolodny, "Matrix Organization Designs and New Product Success," *Research Management,* September 1980, pp. 29–33.

14. Stanley M. Davis and Paul R. Lawrence, *Matrix* (Reading, Mass.: Addison-Wesley, 1977).

15. Kolodny, "Matrix Organization Designs," p. 32.

16. Harold Seneker, "If You Gotta Borrow Money, You Gotta," *Forbes,* April 28, 1980, pp. 116–120.

Index

About the Contributors

Ivars Avots is a member of the senior professional staff of the Arthur D. Little Program Systems Management Company, with principal responsibility for planning and management of international construction projects. Mr. Avots joined Arthur D. Little, Inc., in 1964 after having been recognized as one of the pioneers in the introduction of modern project-management techniques. Since that time, he has advised a variety of companies on the development of systems for managing design and construction of major projects.

Before joining Arthur D. Little, Mr. Avots was president of Management Planning Systems Company, which developed training materials, conducted management-training courses, and provided consulting services in project planning and control techniques. Previously, he was with the Boeing Company, where his initial assignments were in program planning activities during the introduction of the 707 program. Later, he joined the Aero-Space Division planning staff, where he developed divisional operations plans and coordinated the implementation of management systems on major programs.

Mr. Avots received the B.S. in business administration from Susquehanna University and the M.B.A. in industrial management from The Wharton School, University of Pennsylvania. He has lectured and published many articles on project management in the United States and Europe.

David I. Cleland is a professor of systems management engineering in the Department of Industrial Engineering, School of Engineering, University of Pittsburgh. He has authored or coauthored several major books on management and has extensive experience as a lecturer on project management, matrix management, and strategic planning in industrial and governmental organizations.

Dr. Cleland also serves as a director of research projects with the U.S. Department of Agriculture, working on program evaluation for the USDA Combined Forest Pest Research and Development Program. He has consulted for many major industrial organizations, federal and state governmental agencies, military organizations, and educational institutions, and he specializes in the design and operation of project-management systems and strategic-planning systems. He received the B.A. and M.B.A. from the University of Pittsburgh and received the Ph.D. from Ohio State University in 1962.

James Costantino is director of the Transportation Systems Center, the U.S. Department of Transportation's research and development facility for air, highway, rail, pipeline, and marine transportation. He was appointed to this office by the secretary of transportation in January 1976. Dr. Costantino has also served as executive assistant to the deputy secretary of transportation in Washington, D.C., and as regional representative of the Department of Transportation for Federal Region III, based in Philadelphia. Before joining DOT, he worked for nine years with the National Aeronautics and Space Administration as an aerospace engineer in NASA's launch vehicle and propulsion programs and as the director of technical support, Office of Manned Space Flight. He also worked as a mechanical engineer with the Federal Aviation Administration, designing advanced air-traffic-control systems.

Dr. Costantino received the B.S. in mechanical engineering from the University of Massachusetts, the M.A. in engineering administration from George Washington University, and the Ph.D. in transportation policy and economics from American University.

Theodore V. Fowler directs all domestic and international project-finance activities of First Boston Corporation. Before becoming head of the Project Finance Group, he worked in project finance, coordinating the international project-finance activities of the group.

Before joining First Boston in 1976, he worked for the then jointly owned investment banking affiliate of Union Bank of Switzerland and Deutsche Bank, arranging private financing for non-U.S. issuers with operations in the United States. Prior to that he was at Blyth Eastman Dillon, where he worked as a generalist in corporate finance, involved in all areas of public and private financing and advisory work. Mr. Fowler was graduated from Amherst College and Columbia University Graduate School of Business.

Mel Horwitch is assistant professor of management at the Sloan School of Management, Massachusetts Institute of Technology. He received the A.B. from Princeton University and the M.B.A. and Ph.D. from the Harvard Graduate School of Business Administration. He has been a consultant to numerous private firms and public institutions. Dr. Horwitch is the author of many articles and the forthcoming book *Clipped Wings: The American SST Conflict.*

James S. Hoyte is a vice-president of Arthur D. Little Program Systems Management Company. His primary activities involve project management and management consulting pertaining to policy formulation and planning, organizational analysis, transportation-systems management, legal and regulatory analysis, and business planning in a regulatory environment. Mr. Hoyte was secretary-treasurer and director of administration of the Massachusetts Port Authority from 1976 to 1979 and, in 1975, was deputy secretary for commercial affairs and director of corporations for the Commonwealth of Massachusetts.

Mr. Hoyte received the A.B. from Harvard College and the J.D. from Harvard Law School. He completed the Program for Management Development (PMD) at the Harvard Graduate School of Business Administration. He is a member of the Bar of the Commonwealth of Massachusetts and, by appointment of the Massachusetts Superior Court, serves on the Housing Advisory Committee of the Boston Housing Authority.

John F. Magee is president and chief executive officer of Arthur D. Little, Inc. He joined the company in 1950 as a member of the Operations Research Group, of which he became head in January 1959. From 1963 to early 1968, he headed the Management Services Division. Mr. Magee has worked with clients on assignments in marketing research, production planning and inventory control, financial analysis, and economic regulation.

He received the B.A. from Bowdoin College in 1946, the M.B.A. from the Harvard Graduate School of Business Administration in 1948, and the M.A. in mathematics and economics in 1952 from the University of Maine.

Mr. Magee is author of *Production Planning and Inventory Control,* which also has been published in French, Dutch, Japanese, Italian, and Portuguese editions, *Physical Distribution Systems,* and *Industrial Logistics: Analysis and Management of Physical Supply and Distribution Systems.* He has contributed to many other texts and is the author of several technical papers and survey articles in the fields of management and management science.

Peter W.G. Morris has worked for Arthur D. Little, Inc., on a wide variety of projects, including coal, oil, and nuclear-power stations; city-center redevelopment; oil platforms; and steel, petrochemicals, telecommunications, aerospace, and institutional development projects in Europe, North Africa, the Middle East, and South and North America. He specializes in project management, particularly project planning, organization, and control. Before joining Arthur D. Little, he worked for Sir Robert McAlpine, the large U.K. civil-engineering contractors.

Dr. Morris is a frequent lecturer at universities in the United States and Europe and is the author of more than twenty professional papers. He received the B.Sc. in civil engineering in 1968, the M.Sc. in construction management in 1970, and the Ph.D. in project management in 1972, all from Manchester University, England.

C.K. Prahalad is associate professor of policy and control at the University of Michigan Graduate School of Business Administration. He received the B.Sc. from the University of Madras, a postgraduate degree from the Indian Institute of Management at Ahmedabad, and the D.B.A. from the Harvard Graduate School of Business Administration. His teaching, research, and consulting interests are in strategic management and control in large, complex organizations. Dr. Prahalad has published articles in such publications as *Sloan Management Review, Harvard Business Review,* and *Economic and Political Weekly.* He is the coauthor of *Financial Management of Health Institutions* and *The Management of Health Care.*

Stephen W. Ritterbush is a member of the senior professional staff of the Arthur D. Little Program Systems Management Company. He has worked abroad for many years in a wide variety of energy and natural-resource development projects in Southeast Asia, Southern Africa, Europe, and the South Pacific.

Before joining Arthur D. Little, Inc., Dr. Ritterbush was a Rockefeller Foundation Fellow at the Center for Science and International Affairs, John F. Kennedy School of Government, Harvard University. In this capacity he examined the problems associated with large international businesses involved with energy, minerals, and natural resources. He also was a consultant to the Study Commission on U.S. Policy toward Southern Africa and was responsible for conducting an assessment of the energy requirements of the Southern Africa region for the commission. Before working at Harvard University, Dr. Ritterbush served as program coordinator for an autonomous international institute established by The Rockefeller Foundation to promote the exploitation of natural resources in Southeast Asia and the islands of the Pacific Basin. In this capacity, he was a consultant to the region's governments, assisting in the formulation and implementation of their joint-venture resource-development programs.

Dr. Ritterbush received the Ph.D. in economics and the M.A. in international law and diplomacy from the Fletcher School of Law and Diplomacy, Tufts University; the M.S. in oceanography from the University of Hawaii; and the B.S. in civil engineering and the B.A. in political science from Union College. He also spent a year in residence at the University of Stockholm.

Robert C. Seamans, Jr., became Henry R. Luce Professor of Environment and Public Policy at the Massachusetts Institute of Technology in July 1977 and dean of engineering in July 1978. He received the B.S. from Harvard University and the M.S. in aeronautics and the D.S. in instrumentation from the Massachusetts Institute of Technology.

Before returning to MIT, Dr. Seamans was administrator of the Energy

Research and Development Administration (ERDA). He took office at ERDA in December 1974, after serving as president of The National Academy of Engineering, a post to which he was elected in May 1973. From February 1969 until 1973, Dr. Seamans was secretary of the Air Force. Prior to that he was with the National Aeronautics and Space Administration, where he served as associate administrator from September 1960 until December 1965, and then as deputy administrator until 1968.

From 1941 to 1955 he held teaching and project positions at MIT, working on aeronautical developments for instrumentation and control of airplanes and missiles. Dr. Seamans joined Radio Corporation of America (RCA) in 1955 and in 1958 became chief engineer of the Missile Electronics and Controls Division at RCA in Burlington, Massachusetts, a position he held until joining NASA in September 1960. After serving at NASA for more than seven years, Dr. Seamans resigned in January 1968 to become a visiting professor at MIT and in July 1968 was appointed to the Jerome Clarke Hunsaker professorship, an MIT endowed visiting professorship in the Department of Aeronautics and Astronautics.

Allen Sykes is an economist and the group financial director of Willis Faber, Ltd. After five years in the Economics Department of Unilever, in 1960 he joined what became the largest British-based international mining company, RTZ, as head of project evaluation. He was concerned with project evaluation, risk analysis, negotiating long-term sales contracts, and optimization and financing on RTZ projects, which were the largest in the world. As Willis Faber's financial director, he has undertaken considerable advisory work on large international projects and has also been involved in numerous major mining and oil-company arbitrations. He has lectured widely, has published many papers, and has coauthored three books with A.J. Merrett, including *The Finance and Analysis of Capital Projects*.

John R. White is the Arthur D. Little, Inc., senior vice-president for strategic-planning practice, working with staff and clients in the development and application of strategic-planning principles in the United States, Europe, Latin America, and Japan.

Before joining Arthur D. Little, Mr. White held engineering, marketing, and general-management positions in the aircraft, industrial-equipment, and instrumentation fields. He received the B.S. and the M.S. from the California Institute of Technology.

Karl M. Wiig is head of the Systems and Policy Analysis Unit within the Operations Research Section of Arthur D. Little, Inc. His work has focused on applications of systems science to commercial and public-sector problems. He has worked extensively in planning for effective operation of complex systems and in analyses of long-range decision situations.

Before joining Arthur D. Little, Mr. Wiig was manager of systems engineering for a major process company. He was responsible for operations-research projects and for design and implementation of computer-control and plant-information systems.

Mr. Wiig received the B.S. in mechanical engineering and the M.S. in instrumentation from Case Institute of Technology. He is the author or coauthor of many articles on applied systems analysis, decision analysis, and control theory and coauthor (with F. Mansvelt Beck) of *The Economics of Offshore Oil and Gas Supplies* (Lexington Books, 1977).

About the Editor

Albert J. Kelley is president of Arthur D. Little Program Systems Management Company, with responsibility for supervision and management of large, complex projects and developments. Before joining Arthur D. Little, Inc., Dr. Kelley was dean of the School of Management of Boston College. In this capacity, he also was a consultant to public and private organizations and developed seminars on management of technology organizations, project management, long-range planning, and entrepreneurship. He is the author of many articles and coauthor of *Venture Capital: A Guidebook for New Enterprises.*

Before his affiliation with Boston College, Dr. Kelley served with the National Aeronautics and Space Administration (NASA) as program manager of the Agena Vehicle Program, director of electronics and control, and deputy director of the NASA Electronics Research Center. He was also deputy director of the NASA Ad Hoc Manned Lunar Landing Study, which led to Project Apollo. He was awarded the NASA Exceptional Service Medal for these activities.

Dr. Kelley was graduated from the U.S. Naval Academy and received the Sc.D. in engineering from the Massachusetts Institute of Technology. He also completed the Executive Management Program at the University of Minnesota, and the Advanced Management Institute at Carnegie-Mellon University.

Dr. Kelley is a director of the National Space Institute and a member of the Space Applications Board of the National Academy of Engineering. He has served as a White House advisor and as chairman of the Board of Economic Advisors of the Commonwealth of Massachusetts.